Evangelizing Neopagan North America

Evangelizing Neopagan North America

The Word That Frees

Alfred C. Krass

Foreword by Orlando Costas

Institute of Mennonite Studies (IMS)
Missionary Studies, No. 9

HERALD PRESS
Scottdale, Pennsylvania
Kitchener, Ontario
1982

Library of Congress Cataloging in Publication Data

Krass, Alfred C., 1936-
    Evangelizing neopagan North America.

    (Missionary studies; no. 9)
    Includes bibliographical references.
    Appendixes (p.   ): Frankfurt Declaration of the
Fundamental Crisis in Christian Mission (March 1970)—
A Declaration of Evangelical Social Concern (November 25,
1973) — The Lausanne Covenant (1974) — [etc.]
    1. Evangelistic work. I. Title. II. Series.
BV3790.K68 1982   269'.2   81-23768
ISBN 0-8361-1989-4 (pbk.)   AACR2

Scripture quotations from the Revised Standard Version of the Bible,
copyrighted 1946, 1952, © 1971, 1973.

EVANGELIZING NEOPAGAN NORTH AMERICA
Copyright © 1982 by Herald Press, Scottdale, Pa. 15683
    Published simultaneously in Canada by Herald Press,
    Kitchener,Ont. N2G 4M5
Library of Congress Catalog Card Number: 81-23768
International Standard Book Number: 0-8361-1989-4
Printed in the United States of America
Design: Alice B. Shetler

82 83 84 85 86 87 10 9 8 7 6 5 4 3 2 1

This book is dedicated to the
memory of Karl Barth,
the keenness of whose mind
was excelled only by the warm
example of his humanity,
and to
the Brothers of Taizé,
ecumenists *par excellence*,
my partners in prayer these many years.

Contents

Foreword

This is a provocative book by a stimulating author. It marks a further step in the author's pilgrimage toward a contextually critical and evangelically radical understanding of evangelism in North America. Those who have followed Krass's previous works will be pleased or disappointed with this one; they will not be neutral.

Already in *Beyond the Either-Or Church* (Nashville: Tidings, 1973) Krass referred to North America as a mission field. He stated then that "in any situation where people do not know to whom they belong there is a mission field ..." (p. 68) and the United States was in this regard no better off than the most heathen parts of the globe. Krass's concern then was for the recovery of the wholeness of evangelism in America. He continued this same concern in *Five Lanterns at Sundown: Evangelism in a Chastened Mood* (Grand Rapids: Eerdmans, 1978). However, whereas in the former he was trying to stimulate the conscience of the church to the needs and opportunities for evangelism against the defeatist and pessimistic attitude of the 60s, in the latter he took a more sober look at a ministry that had been recovered in many churches but without its cutting edge, portraying an attitude of hope subdued by a realistic assessment of middle-class North American society.

Evangelizing Neopagan North America reflects a further, more critical look. The question now is not simply one of a church that has forgotten the holistic imperative of evangelism nor that of a complacent middle-class society, but rather that of a narcissistic culture, a practically atheistic region which is part of a demonic capitalistic world. For Krass evangelism in such a situation involves a more concrete reading of Jesus' evangelistic approach, a more critical understanding of the problems of religion and culture, of idolatry and power in the Western world, and the development of a style of evangelism which arises out of a community which lives out the message of God's grace, proclaims and celebrates the gospel, is concerned with the specific problems of women and men, and is oriented toward the transformation of human history into the new creation.

The book is historically situated at the end of a decade (the seventies) that witnessed a renewed interest in evangelism around the world. It is understandable, therefore, that the author would undertake an analysis of evangelism in this period. He concludes that the seventies produced a new understanding of evangelism but left an unfinished agenda. As evidence, he includes eleven appendices containing the most ecumenically significant statements on evangelism of the decade. That in itself is worth the whole book.

For Krass, however, the seventies was a continuum of the pilgrimage initiated by him as a missionary in West Africa in the 1960s. Therefore, he engages in a critical evaluation of his self-understanding as a missionary during this period. In so doing, he sets the stage for his new evangelistic context which is neither that of consultant in a mainline Protestant missionary society (the 70s) nor that of a white missionary in black Africa (the 60s), but rather that of a member of an ecumenical community of white Christians from a middle-class background which have opted to live in an integrated neighborhood and evangelize, as it were, from "below,"—from the perspective of the powerless, the poor, and the oppressed. This does not mean that he has now abandoned the global perspective that shaped his earlier writings. On the contrary, this new context has deepened his identification with the Third World and has made it more authentic. For by becoming part of a powerless white minority that has decided to pitch its tent among the poor and oppressed North American minorities, Al Krass has not only become a committed Christian. He has also been able to strengthen his solidarity with the Third World and has deepened his quest for a liberating contextual evangelism in North America.

I welcome this book as a testimony of how God is liberating for service a minority of Christians in mainstream North American society. I salute the author for his evangelistic authenticity. I give thanks to God for his prophetic courage and the challenge of his book. May it be received thoughtfully and prayerfully by Christians everywhere, but especially in North America.

Orlando E. Costas
Eastern Baptist Theological Seminary
Philadelphia, Pennsylvania
Christmas 1981

Preface

In this volume the Institute of Mennonite Studies makes available two important contributions to the topic of evangelism—Krass's essays and the extensive appendices. Evangelism, according to the burden of this book, calls people to accept a gospel that confronts the demons which rule our society, including popular perversions of Christianity that prostitute the gospel for political and psychological securities. Evangelism invites people to become *a new creation*, disciples who model kingdom values.

Alfred Krass's essays, presented originally at the Associated Mennonite Biblical Seminary as the 1979-80 Theological Lectures combined with the meeting of the Mennonite Missionary Study Fellowship, represent a missionary's pilgrimage on this issue during the seventies. Learning from overseas perspectives (chapter 2), Krass's testimony focuses upon the North American scene. What does evangelism mean at home, in modern America, evaluated as a neopagan society?

The maximal use of this book will be achieved when the reader, driven by Spirit-desire to witness to the gospel, asks: How do these perspectives and learnings impact my de-

nomination, my congregation, and me in commitment and
effort to proclaim and live the gospel? How do I witness to
Jesus Christ in my neopagan local community? Am I ready
to invite people into my congregation of faith and with them
walk the way to the kingdom of God?

Krass's writing will surely test and challenge every
reader's understandings; some readers may find themselves
wanting to describe America's neopaganism differently or to
redefine evangelism. To be sure, in this book Krass helps us
rethink the evangelistic task, spurring us forward to a fuller
vision of the missionary calling of God's people at home, our
neopagan society.

Perhaps a demurrer on the word neopagan is in order. It
does not describe simply the rise of the cults, although their
success within North American society plays into Krass's
thesis. Nor does the term mean to indicate that North
America is returning to primal religion. Rather, as Krass
points out, neopaganism here describes a North American
society whose "mess of pottage" smells and tastes psuedo-
Christian, even anti-Christian. In the name of psychological
comfort and political self-interest, narcissism and political
triumphalism rule us, making even our version of the Christian gospel their serfs.

The eleven appendices represent the Christian churches'
tensions, dialogue, and development on the same theme
during the 1970-1980 decade. All the voices in the appendices, representing a wide Christian spectrum,
Protestant and Roman Catholic, demonstrate a struggle to
grasp the contemporary evangelistic task to which God calls
the faithful church; the struggle is an issue of faith and
conscience, belief and behavior. From this rich ecumenical
legacy, John Stott sees a converging of understanding and
emphases (see Appendix 9).

While some of these eleven statements represent the "official" voice of church groups and others speak for ad hoc groups of concern, we might ask, as Krass does, What were the congregations doing in the seventies? How many congregations or denominational policy executives were strategizing and carrying out evangelistic endeavors which called people to the liberating gospel of the kingdom—personally, socially, economically, and politically? Or were the churches acquiescing to the values and structures of their society—which, alas, we are here told, is neopagan? However we evaluate the seventies, the challenge of the eighties lies before us. How will we respond?

With gratitude, I acknowledge the numerous publishers and people who gave permission to print the appendices. I thank also Charmaine Jeschke who assisted me in the editing of the manuscript, Jean Kelly and Sue Yoder for typing the manuscript, and Herald Press book editor, Paul M. Schrock. Most of all, I am grateful to Al Krass for this important contribution to a topic of top priority on the church's agenda.

Willard M. Swartley, Director
Institute of Mennonite Studies
November 1981

Introduction

If we believe evangelism must be appropriate to the people we evangelize and the times they live in, as I do, writing a book about it seems like trying to hit a moving target.

When I consider the changes which have come about in the United States since the lectures on which this book is based were delivered in 1980, it seems brash to attempt to publish the book and consider it still relevant. Scores of commentators have told us that the shift from the Carter to the Reagan administrations was one of the major shifts in U.S. history. How then can what was written in the last days of Carter apply to evangelism in the present time?

My Mennonite associates have insisted that the manuscript is still relevant. With each successive reading I have become convinced that they are right. I wonder why this is the case. Is it that the atmosphere of the Associated Mennonite Biblical Seminaries and of the Mennonite Missionary Study Fellowship breathed an Anabaptist spirit that kept me from identifying any administration too closely with the kingdom? (I have seldom been in a place where Christians sat more loosely with the culture of which they are a part!) Or is it that my theological and sociological analysis made me see the Carter administration as far less benign than in retrospect it seems?

We're tempted now to romanticize the past—the days of Carter, Johnson's Great Society, the New and Fair Deals. By contrast, we're tempted to diabolize the present. But as Christians alone, if not as social analysts, we all ought to recognize that the administrations we have had, different though they are, are variants of one basic model. A Chevy is, for sure, not a Ford. Nor is a Ford a Plymouth. But the products of our three leading car manufacturers differ from one another more in style than in substance.

The same is true of our governments. No administration we have known in the post-War years has basically altered the distribution of power and wealth in our society. Sociological statistics depressingly demonstrate how little things have changed in this century.

Power in our society, under Carter as under Reagan, belongs to the few. The military-industrial-scientific complex, whose creature many see Reagan to be, influenced Carter as much as it does Reagan. Militarism has held unquestioned sway over our nation's policies since 1948 at least.

If we have a "massive military build-up" at this time in our history, it's but a small increment to what was already established as the norm far earlier. If we have a decline in the income of the poor and tax relief for the rich, we must remember that the rich have never been subject to a truly graduated tax structure in our society, and we have only helped the poor when it's been clearly in the interest of the rich that we do so.

Since that's the case, evangelism as conceived now isn't going to be very different from evangelism as conceived in 1980. Societies do not change that quickly. It is as urgent to bring people to a consciousness of the radical distnace of the present order of North American society from the kingdom now as it was then. It is as necessary to awaken people to the dream of God's in-breaking order now as it was in more "liberal" times. At both points it falls to us with equal urgency to mobilize those who hear the evangel to become part of dynamic communities of prayer and resistance, of hope and liberating action.

That's a long way from saying that evangelism is everywhere and at every time the same. Though Jesus Christ is "the same yesterday, today, and forever" (Heb. 13:8), how we present him to different societies or to the same society at different points dare not be the same. Christ is risen, alive, and very much present in his Spirit in each one and at each time, and where we see Christ present will determine how we call people to be his disciples.

At Associated Mennonite Biblical Seminaries and in the Mennonite Mission Study Fellowship I found a company of people wonderfully open to understand the newness of God's workings, ready to explore in a disciplined way the specificity of today's evangelistic and pastoral task. My gratitude goes out to both bodies for the faith they placed in me by inviting me to deliver these lectures. The finished book owes no small debt to the ways they, in the ensuing discussion, helped me recognize the weak points and reinforce the strengths of the lectures.

Particular thanks goes to Wilbert Shenk, director of Overseas Missions at the Mennonite Board of Missions, and Willard Swartley, director of the Institute of Mennonite Studies. Shenk discerned the unity behind what I had been writing in separate contexts about mission at home and mission abroad and asked me to develop this further. Swartley helped me refine the plan for the lectures and develop them into a coherent book. He and his capable assistants edited and provided background material for the volume.

Along the way many others contributed to what I here present: the participants in the Lausanne Committee for World Evangelization's 1978 Willowbank Consultation, those at the World Council of Churches' Evangelism Consultation at Bossey in 1979, and those at various Theology in the Americas meeting in which I shared. So also the academic institutions at which parts of these lectures were originally given: Perkins School of Theology, McMaster Divinity School, and Illinois Wesleyan University. A day with the ministers of the Chicago Metropolitan Association of the United Church of Christ was extremely helpful, as was a weekend with Koinonia Partners.

My regular partners in dialogue helped with this book as they have before—Orlando Costas, Isaac Rottenberg, Douglas Meeks, Peter Henriot, and Joe Holland. Anne McGlinchey of the National Institute for Lay Training encouraged me, and its students raised many questions.

Thanks must also be given to the members of the Evangelism Working Group of the National Council of Churches, for whom I served as consultant from 1977 to 1979. Finally I was stimulated by the open discussion at the Ventnor Mission Study Group under Dr. Gerald Anderson.

For the sociological analysis I recognize once again my indebtedness to my teacher, the late Benjamin Nelson. Though not a Christian, he understood the radical nature of the Christian message much better than most of us Christians.

All along the way, however, it was the members of Jubilee Fellowship and the staff at *The Other Side* who provided the lived-in context out of which these reflections developed.

The shortcomings of the work are my own.

Alfred C. Krass
Philadelphia, Pennsylvania

Evangelizing Neopagan North America

CHAPTER 1

Evangelism: Casting Out
the Demons

They came to the other side of the sea, to the country of the Gerasenes. And when he had come out of the boat, there met him out of the tombs a man with an unclean spirit, who lived among the tombs; and no one could bind him any more, even with a chain; for he had often been bound with fetters and chains, but the chains he wrenched apart, and the fetters he broke in pieces; and no one had the strength to subdue him. Night and day among the tombs and on the mountains he was always crying out, and bruising himself with stones. And when he saw Jesus from afar, he ran and worshiped him; and crying out with a loud voice, he said, "What have you to do with me, Jesus, Son of the Most High God? I adjure you by God, do not torment me." For he had said to him, "Come out of the man, you unclean spirit!" And Jesus asked him, "What is your name?" He replied, "My name is Legion; for we are many." And he begged him eagerly not to send them out of the country. Now a great herd of swine was feeding there on the hillside; and they begged him, "Send us to the swine, let us enter them." So he gave them leave. And the unclean spirits came out, and entered the swine; and the herd, numbering about two thousand, rushed down the steep bank into the sea, and were drowned in the sea.

The herdsmen fled, and told it in the city and in the country. And people came to see what it was that had happened. And they came to Jesus, and saw the demoniac sitting there, clothed and in his right mind, the man who had had the legion; and they were afraid. And those who had seen it told what had happened to the demoniac and to the swine. And they began to beg Jesus to depart from their neighborhood.

Mark 5:1-17

O f all the bizarre stories in the New Testament, which one could be less appropriate to apply to the people of our secularized contemporary world than this? An exorcism of a man possessed by so many demons that he believed he had a whole legion of them—demons who spoke, who appealed to Jesus, "Don't send us out of the country!" The strange beliefs about swine, about "clean" and "unclean" animals, and about demons rushing into the swine which, once possessed, rush madly down the steep bank to drown in the lake. And no questions raised by the author about the ethics of Jesus either—how he could cause those harmless creatures to die that way!

An impossible story.

Perhaps we think we're sophisticated. Seventeen years ago I heard a Ghanaian professor preach to a prep school congregation in that West African country. He apologized for the story's crudeness. He assumed they couldn't believe it. (A footnote: they did.)

Now I'm sure the story has remained accessible to many people in our country as well—people who take the Bible literally, people who aren't disturbed by the claims of modern science. I'm prepared to accept that some people who are "into" exorcisms could take it pretty much at face value. I have a strong sense of the historical faithfulness of the Scriptures and a belief in their authority for Christian life and faith. Nevertheless, for many years I had to see this story as legendary in some of its details. Though I could grant that an "exorcism" took place, I demythologized it. It must have been something, I reasoned, like rapid-fire psychotherapy. There weren't actually any demons present. The man had a personality which was split many ways. He suffered from such total personality disassociation that he didn't know who he was. Jesus, I reasoned, spoke an authoritative word which restored his sense of self and cured him of his schizophrenia, as it were. In the process of the cure the man shrieked so loudly that he frightened the pigs into running into the lake.

I maintained the "essence" of the story, I thought. The man was cured. A raving madman became whole; he returned to what Mark called "his right mind." Furthermore, the cure amazed the Gerasenes. They sensed an eerie power in Jesus. They were uncomfortable, so they asked him to leave their land.

Only recently have I come to value the whole of this miracle-healing story and not feel that I have to swallow hard to accept it. I no longer demythologize it, and for two reasons.

1. For the first time I stopped to ask who it was that asked Jesus to leave the country. Mark doesn't tell us directly. Notice, it doesn't happen right away. The original witnesses—rough, simple herdsmen—weren't the ones who told Jesus to leave. Their reaction was to run into town and report what had happened.

Why? You would have, too! If you were herding two thousand hogs and all of a sudden they were gone—dead—lost, your employers would want to know what had happened to them. At that point your job security would be pretty low.

I'm sure the herdsmen didn't rush into town to report the miraculous cure. They ran to report the loss of their employers' fortune. Although, to the Jews, the loss of "unclean" hogs meant nothing, the Gerasenes regarded hogs much the way an Indiana farmer does—as money.

This Jew, Jesus, from across the lake had made a fundamental attack on their way of making money, their economic system. How much money would two thousand hogs be worth nowadays? Not a small sum. It wasn't then either.

I began to suspect that what drove the people to tell Jesus to leave was much less a sense of the sacred than the loss of their capital investment. Over and over again in the Gospels and the Acts, Jesus' and the apostles' attack on commercial power gets the people terribly riled up. There were the money changers in the temple (see Matthew 21:12-13) and the silversmiths of Ephesus too (see Acts 19:23-27). The silversmiths became riotous when Paul started telling the Ephesians to stop believing in idols. Their stock-in-trade was silver models of the temple of Artemis in Ephesus. That shrine brought many, many tourists to the city. The silversmiths' leader, Demetrius, correctly reasoned that Paul would not only bring the cult of Artemis into disrepute. He would also ruin their livelihood. In fact, over time, Demetrius was right.

So notice what the silversmiths did—they inspired a popular riot. They got Paul and his companions into the great amphitheater. For the next two hours the scene may have resembled the events in Iran in 1979 when students first seized the hostages at the U.S. Embassy in Teheran. Biblical faith, I recognized, threatens certain types of entrenched economic power. When I remembered that, I began to realize that the story of the healing of Legion had more to say than I had expected.

It did in another way, too. The story has significance in the culture of Roman colonialism in the Eastern Mediterranean. As Elizabeth Schüssler Fiorenza has observed,

> . . . the demon in Mark 5:1-13 is called Legion, with the same name as the Roman soldiers who occupied Palestine. The story presents an irony of the Roman exploitation when it has the demon expelled into a herd of pigs, animals that were, for Jewish sensitivities, the paradigm of ritual impurity. Miracle-faith is here protest against bodily and political suffering. It gives courage to resist all life-destroying power of one's society.[1]

2. After reading Christopher Lasch's book, *The Culture of Narcissism*,[2] I began to take the story more seriously. Now I know that narcissism and schizophrenia aren't the same thing. But a lot of what Lasch writes about in his book isn't just about narcissism, but about a more general problem: how the mental illnesses of individuals are often related to the problems of society. Mentally ill people are only the most extreme cases of what the culture as a whole is experiencing.

I will go into Lasch's book in fair detail in chapter 5. But here I want to suggest that the story of the healing of Legion is a suggestive paradigm of what happens in evangelism in our culture today.

First, when we evangelize, we are performing a certain kind of exorcism. Second, Legion's condition was in many respects like the condition of our society today. Third, the reaction of the hog owners is like the reaction we meet when we really evangelize—people don't want us around. Fourth, when an exorcism occurs, people are healed. Their isolation is overcome; their alienation is done away with. Fifth, those who are healed are restored to community, the community

God intended us to live in. To put it all together, evangelism is the work of God's kingdom.

We've become so used to separating evangelism from the kingdom and to interpreting evangelism in privatized, "spiritual" terms that we don't usually connect it with the kingdom. We forget that the object of the verb *euangelizomai* (to announce "good news") is, in the synoptic Gospels, the kingdom. We forget that the content of the noun *euangelion* (the good news) is the kingdom, the announcement that in Jesus Christ the kingdom has entered human history.

At the Lausanne Congress on World Evangelization in 1974 a lively debate took place over whether any connection exists between evangelism and the kingdom. Only for Jews, some people answered. When the gospel message went out to Samaria and to the Gentiles, it wasn't the kingdom that was preached, but Jesus Christ. Rene Padilla argued forcefully and, I believe, biblically that no such dichotomy exists in the New Testament. He argued that all New Testament evangelism is kingdom evangelism. The word studies which I have done since that time have convinced me that Padilla was right. There is no hiatus in the Bible between the mission to Israel (the Jews) and the mission to the rest of the world—such as that once Jesus Christ became the content of the good news, the kingdom was no longer preached. The kingdom always remained central.

But what helped me even more was an insight Emilio Castro shared with us at the World Council of Churches' Workshop on Evangelism at Bossey in June 1979. The reason Paul didn't generally speak of the kingdom of God was that he was an effective cross-cultural missionary. He knew he had to translate that term so that it would speak to a Gentile audience. Therefore he didn't speak of the kingdom but of *dikaiosune,* justice (or, as the earlier translations have it, righteousness). The content of his preaching was the justice of God—an event, a happening, something coming into history and transforming it. But that's how the Jews understood the kingdom.

Although the early church understood *dikaiosune* dynamically, more and more over the course of the church's history, *dikaiosune* came to be interpreted as an attribute of God or as an individual virtue—righteousness. Paul's cosmic eschatology gave way to a dehistoricized, individual, salvation-or-damnation eschatology. Adept though the Reformers were at recapturing much of the original thrust of the New Testament, they failed on this point. They maintained a sub-biblical eschatology. Nevertheless John Calvin sowed the seeds for a renewed, full-orbed biblical eschatology. In our own day Reformed theologians have brought those seeds to maturity. Similarly the Radical Reformation recovered much of what had been lost for centuries in its renewed sense of the dynamic thrust of eschatology.

In our own time, however, it is probably within the Roman Catholic Church, through the Second Vatican Council and the development of the theology of liberation, (see Appendix 6) that evangelism and eschatology have been rescued most fully from their otherworldly imprisonment. The renewal of the Anabaptist movement, the development of new Reformed approaches, and the emergence of liberation theology—different though these processes are—have brought us to a new sense of the relationship of evangelism to the kingdom. The analysis I use in this and subsequent chapters owes much to each of these streams.

How do we understand the world in which we live? Let me answer for myself. I get up in the morning. I listen to the news on the radio. I read the newspaper. I take my son out to the school bus. A neighbor is passing by. I greet her. I learn what happened at the community meeting last night. I make a call to check on what's happened with the Philadelphia Council of Neighborhood Organizations' protest against red-lining practices. I open the morning's mail—a call to a meeting on energy concerns for poor citizens, a request to convene a task force to look into the abuse of ex-mental patients by boarding home operators, and an emergency meeting on school desegregation.

I go to the office of *The Other Side*. Along the way I pass a long-abandoned house. It has a new sign on it: "This house is being renovated by the Southwest Germantown Community Development Corporation." I continue down the street. I see that the Park Commission's trucks and crew are on the job. Hallelujah! They're cleaning up the vacant lot our church reclaimed from the junkies last summer! Through many days of work, we'd humanized it again. Now the Park Commission has finally accepted the responsibility to change the lot into the public park its owner had intended it to be when he died and willed it to the city a dozen years ago.

I sit at my desk in the office. A whole load of mail. "Please give some publicity to the campaign to stop the Olympic Prison." "Could you inform your readers that there's going to be a consultation on urban mission in Chicago next month?" "The Coalition Against Registration and the Draft is calling people to make their protests known." "We're forming a new Christian community in Springfield. Can you let your readers know?"

My head is spinning. Time for a coffee break. Let all this soak in a bit. The verse I had read from Ephesians earlier comes to mind: "We are appointed to live for his praise and glory." I think of the new park. I think of the community in

Springfield. I think of the coalition against the draft. I think of the campaign to stop the Olympic Prison. I remember a conversation with Steve Angell, one of its leaders.

"What kind of hope do you have?" I had asked him when he visited last year. "Do you really hope that you can abolish prisons?"

"I guess I have the same hope Pastorius had," this Quaker responds, "when he worked for the abolition of slavery. It took a hundred years before the Friends' Yearly Meeting came to agree with him. Then it took another hundred before slavery was abolished. Change doesn't come quickly." Plenty to think about there.

The way I understand God's Word is through a process which I have just described. All day long I read and reflect on the Word, by myself and in community. Where is God working today? How do I understand what God is doing? As the report of the Willowbank Consultation on "The Gospel and Culture," which I attended two years ago puts it:

> The task of understanding the Scriptures belongs not just to individuals but to the whole Christian community, seen as both a contemporary and a historical fellowship. . . .

> The Holy Spirit instructs his people through a variety of teachers of both the past and the present. We need each other. It is only "with all the saints" that we can begin to comprehend the full dimensions of God's love (Ephesians 3:18-19). The Spirit illumines the minds of God's people in every culture to perceive . . . the Scripture's truth freshly through their own eyes and thus discloses to the whole church ever more of the many colored wisdom of God, as the Lausanne Covenant puts it.[3]

It's a hard task to discern what God is doing today. I rejoice that, as I walk through Germantown and live in

Philadelphia, I do not have to discern God's action all on my own. First I have the brothers and sisters in my own church community, Jubilee Fellowship, to guide me. Then I have the voices of the other churches in our community and beyond—the witness of Christians in Europe, Latin America, Asia and Africa. I also have the witness of the church down through the ages.

I do all my discernment as part of a community. The central context of that community's life, its central act, the Lord's supper or Eucharist, is the center out of which I and my brothers and sisters operate. In regular observance of the Lord's supper we celebrate the triumph of life over death, of resurrection over crucifixion. We reaffirm that this is God's world, that God is working to redeem it from its sin and alienation. That's a fantastic assurance, an unbelievable gift. The table of the Lord's supper is also the place where we offer ourselves to God over and over again, to serve the kingdom as we are strengthened by the power of the Holy Spirit.

As disciples we call others to discipleship. We invite them into the fellowship of the crucified and risen Lord. What we have to offer them, as Ans van der Bent puts it in his recent book, *God So Loves the World*[4], is that "in the shadow of the cross we will together continue to share and to combat domination, exploitation, greed, and selfishness." We'll do it with hope, because God has promised us that "all partly achieved community among human beings will ultimately be liberated and fulfilled."

"The shadow of the cross"—I see it so clearly. How can you avoid it if you look at the world as it is? "Our defense spending is running amok," Congressman Bill Gray said in a meeting at the First United Methodist Church of Germantown in early 1980. "We feel we have to buy any new gadget or toy which becomes available. But to buy them we're mortgaging the future of all our people. We can't begin to deal with the problems we face in New York, Philadelphia, or rural Iowa because we're taking the limited resources we have and putting them into kill-power the U.S. doesn't need."

"We're tied to the belief," Congressman Gray said, "that our economy cannot function without the military-industrial complex, that what makes a nation strong is its bombs and bullets, not what's within it—its justice and equity. We are tied to this false belief because those who are informed and know it's a myth don't spend as much time organizing and lobbying as do those who support the illusions."

"Because of what we're spending on defense," Gordon Cosby said at the same meeting, "it's becoming increasingly difficult for us to maintain our way of life. We've basically decided that, with that much pressure on the lives of most Americans, we simply can't afford to look after the bottom 20 percent anymore. That's forty million Americans that we're saying we can't look after! We'll tolerate whatever happens to them, but we won't question the defense budget."

At this same time Governor Thornburgh introduced legislation to cut half the people off the Pennsylvania welfare rolls. With unemployment at 8 percent, he says, "The able-bodied people can get jobs." The Black Caucus is trying to filibuster the proposal to death, but will it work? The white legislators, even the liberals among them, are feeling that we simply can't afford to spend so much money on welfare anymore.

For every 100,000 additional people unemployed, over 260 more crimes will be committed, a Penn State sociologist has discovered. Yet we believe that we can tolerate increased unemployment. This will result in less security, more arrests, more people imprisoned, more crowded prisons, more prison riots, more families torn apart, and more racial stress. Yet we are willing to go along with those proposals.

We're willing to go along with an economy that is increasingly directed by the power of large corporations, companies like the Lykes Corporation which simply shut down its Youngstown Steel plant, throwing five thousand people out of work, depressing the whole Mahoning Valley.

We seem to think that there is a kind of parallel democracy which operates in the economic realm. Shareholders, we believe, tell directors what to do; directors tell management. "Look how many people own shares in General Motors and ITT," we say. "Americans own their corporations." But in reality, as those who have introduced the Corporate Democracy Act in Congress point out,[5] this image is virtually a myth:

> In nearly every large American business corporation, there exists a management autocracy. One man . . . or a small coterie of men rule the corporation.

> Although the board of directors is theoretically the "legislature" of the corporation, checking and balancing the "executive" officers—they're actually handpicked by the officers because they mirror their interests. . . .

> Directors do not select the top officers, do not establish company objectives, strategies or policies, do not possess the information necessary to make such judgments, and rarely if ever dissent from managerial initiatives. . . .

> Shareholders too are relatively powerless. Because management controls the proxy machinery, because shareholders cannot nominate candidates for the board, because individual shareholders are overwhelmed by the bloc voting of shares of

institutional investors, they play a ceremonial role in corporate governance.... Few shareholders personally attend meetings.... Even "Campaign GM," the most publicized shareholder challenge of the past two decades, attracted no more than 3,000 of General Motors' 1,400,000 shareholders, or roughly two-tenths of one percent.... In 1973, 99.7 percent of the elections for directors in our largest corporations were uncontested.[6]

But our alienation is not only seen in relation to the military and the corporations. The realm of unfreedom extends to all of our lives. In a recent article psychologists Tom Ludwig and David Myers wrote about what motivates Americans in terms of lifestyle, what influences their everyday decisions, and what lies behind their economic values:

Our feelings of satisfaction and dissatisfaction are always relative to our prior experience. If our current achievements are below those of the past, we feel frustrated. If they're above, we feel satisfied. This is what we call the "adaptation-level phenomenon." But what happens when you've lived for a while with a new level of achievement, is that you become used to it. What was formerly positive becomes neutral—you expect that level of satisfaction from life. And what was formerly neutral becomes negative.

For this reason, increased material affluence or social prestige gives us only an initial surge of pleasure. Once we raise our level of possessions and material wealth, we initially feel good. But then, soon it becomes neutral. In order to recapture the feeling of happiness and satisfaction, we have to raise our level of possessions again. We're on the treadmill.[7]

On and on it goes—despite the increased pollution of the environment it causes, despite the increased use of energy and natural resources, and despite the inflation it causes us to suffer. If at any point we could analyze the benefits and liabilities of our constant upward mobility, we would realize that—in terms of pleasure alone—it doesn't pay. But the corporate world, through the media, keeps us from making that analysis. "You deserve a break today," they tell us. "Don't you think you deserve the best?"

At the time of the first oil boycott in 1973, Pierre Emmanuel of the Académie Francaise looked at what the oil nations' new militancy ought to signal for the Western world.

> From the Bandung Conference of 1955: the first display of third world militancy and solidarity, till now, less than twenty years have passed. During these years, technological civilization has experienced tremendously accelerated growth and inflation, thanks to third world primary products. It's strange that, in the space of twenty years, so few responsible decision-makers have questioned the fragility of this spectacular progress in its universal transformations, so overwhelming to human psychology.

> Quite the contrary. In less than a generation we've all formed more new habits and reflexes than we had since the beginning of the industrial age.... We can't do without these new things. We're already conditioned by them. The gigantic system never stops moving. It never relents. Instead it continues to accelerate even more. It risks pushing the Western world to the point of its total destruction.

> It would be an illusion to believe that now all can continue more or less as it did before.... We need to learn how to re-adapt together to the new situation. We need new values, new relationships between persons and nations, new technologies. What we really have to do is "learn how to live all over again."[8]

Several years have now passed without much sign that we've begun to do what Emmanuel called on us to do. What do we make of that? It's hard to resist the conclusion that we are enslaved. Though many people and organizations try to awaken us and try to help us see how dangerous our different slaveries actually are, they don't get through to us.

In February 1980 the producer of Handel's 18th-century oratorio *Judas Maccabaeus* was loudly booed and received death threats. What had he done? He brought a modernized setting of the oratorio to Munich. He had depicted the Hebrew martyrs of the time before Christ as victims of the Nazi Holocaust. Members of the youth chorus wore uniforms of the Hitler Youth Organization. Why did he do this? He said he wanted to show how Handel's work could be made relevant to modern events. He wanted to help people realize how history is controlled by different political and religious forces. But no one wanted to hear this message, he said. They only wanted to hear positive words.[9]

When I went to Pope John Paul II's outdoor mass in Philadelphia in October 1979, I marveled at the pontiff's sense of how to appeal to an American audience. When he quoted the Declaration of Independence, he was cheered loudly. He received great ovations when he spoke of what the vision of Jefferson and the other founding fathers had meant for the world. When he referred to the absence of such freedom and democracy in "some countries," the applause was strong. People nodded their heads with understanding.

I think the crowd heard what he said about the danger of raping the environment. But they didn't applaud. I think they understood when he called on us to see that the poor are not oppressed. But they didn't cheer. These matters did not bring elation.

When the pope went on to speak pastorally about Christian morality in a permissive society, the woman in front of me gasped, "Oh, he's on to that again!" We don't want to hear anything that demands that we change.

"Blessed is he who takes no offense at me," Jesus said. "What an incredibly low level of assent Jesus seems to require here," Ronald Goetz reflects.[10] "Blessed are those who merely don't despise him. Perhaps there is hope—not just for John but even for us. At least we don't take offense at him. Or do we?" he goes on to ask.

> Consider how strange are his apocalyptic views. Clearly his economics, from either a capitalist or a socialist perspective, are a scandal. His teaching on nonresistance to evil would, if taken literally, seem to us North American armchair revolutionaries quite reactionary. He taught about irreversible hell and about taking no heed for the morrow. Let's be honest— we often take offense at him. . . .

> At first glance, these words seemed to open a criterion for fellowship with him; but as we reflect, as we draw near on this open basis, suddenly we are dismayed. These words seem to exclude us. . . .

> His burden is not light, because we cannot bear it and it alone. We want this world, its riches, its power, its pleasures, and we want his yoke as well. . . . So we are drawn to his manifestation and repelled by it, but drawn and drawn again, for we have nowhere else to go. He alone has the works and words of eternal life. . . . Those who are too fascinated, too enthralled to stand back, and who come to him, are awed and appalled by the richness of his signs, and cry with Peter, "Depart from us, Lord, for we are sinful."[11]

It's much easier to have a nonquestioning religion, one that causes no offense, which appeals to all our prejudices and supports our values. We can find such religions in the myriad cults which are open and available to us in our

neopagan society. We can find it in the "Christian" church
as well. A look at the offerings on a Sunday morning TV
screen can give us many alternatives to Jesus' religion. Many
of them come with beautiful Christian frosting. They remind me of the religion offered by the Rev. Doctor Moon (a
prophetic name!), a criminal who is posing as a minister in
Cole Porter's Broadway musical of the thirties, *Anything
Goes*. When asked to give spiritual counsel, he sings the
following song:

> When your instincts tell you disaster
> Is coming faster and faster,
> Be like the bluebird and sing,
> "Tweet, tweet, tweet" . . .
> Be like the bluebird who never is blue.

We seem to be looking for a religion which keeps us from
being blue. Such religions are not a means of liberation but
of continued enjoyment. We are "cultural addicts," Father
Bill Callahan writes, "tied to our culture with a thousand little strands, as effectively fastened down as was Gulliver by
the Lilliputians."[12] Our religions are among those strands,
it's sad to say.

"The Bible wants to be taken," John Howard Yoder
writes, "as power for change"[13] not as continuation of the
status quo. Change we have to recognize brings conflict.
"Because of its contents," Bolivian Methodists declared in
1974,[14] "evangelism is conflictive. It creates a conflict in the
hearer, in the witness, and in society." To announce the
gospel we must denounce everything that is not in
agreement with it:

> No evangelism is authentically evangelical if it is not at the
> same time prophetic. The church cannot compromise with

any force that oppresses or dehumanizes persons. It cannot name Jesus Christ if it does not name also the idols and the demons that must be cast out from the inner lives of persons and from the structures of society.

But such an evangelism, the Bolivians believe, not only casts out demons. It also "sets in motion the human forces of liberation." It "becomes a dynamism in history."

Can evangelism become such a liberating dynamism in the U.S.? Can it liberate us from the destructive force of corporate capitalist autocracy, from the power of militarism? Can it free us from the devastating effects of consumerism?

I see such an evangelism being born again in our time. I see a truly kingdom-oriented evangelism emerging, one which, I predict, will radically reshape what we think of as "church" in the remaining years of this century. I see it in the response of the Ecumenical Coalition of the Mahoning Valley which was formed when Lykes shut down their steel works. "We are profoundly disturbed and troubled by this decision and its tragic consequences," the Coalition announced. Though it did not claim to be a group of "experts in steel production or economic matters" and could not offer "easy answers," it nevertheless felt that, "as pastors deeply concerned about the pain and fear now present in our community," it needed to examine the causes of the crisis and ask how it might act to alleviate the suffering—and restore economic health to the valley. The Coalition wanted to insure that this distress would not happen again.

The Coalition's statement analyzes Lykes' decision as "the result of a way of doing business in this country that too often fails to take into account the human dimensions of economic action." As religious leaders they could not "ignore the moral and religious aspects of this crisis." It was not, they said, a "private, purely economic" matter. Since it affected the lives of all the people of the valley, they saw it "as a matter of public concern." The ministers explained the theological basis for their involvement. Then they went on winsomely to argue that "economic decisions ought not to be left to the judgment of a few persons with economic power, but should be shared with the larger community which is affected."[15]

As a by-product of the Coalition's effort, Christian faith took on new meaning for many people who had tended to write it off. "The Coalition was different from what I've normally seen of the churches," steelworker John McNicol confessed. "Normally," he said, "they don't like to make a whole lot of waves. They try to keep people straight. At first," he relates, "some workers said, 'What's a bunch of ministers doing in this?' " But I remember another steelworker saying to the churches, "You are all we have. If we don't have you behind us, what have we got? I think if the church was more involved in issues like Youngstown," he goes on, "more people would be active in the churches. We need a place where we can walk in, feel this is a united place, speak and be spoken to, and still respect it as the house of God. We need a place where individuals can feel it's not only God's home, but their home. Every church on every corner should be a mission. We should all be missionaries."[16]

I sense a new, kingdom-oriented evangelism in the Pastoral Letter of the Catholic Bishops of Appalachia, issued in 1975.[17] Based in hardheaded social and historical analysis, this remarkable document is a milestone in contextual evangelism. Issued in newspaper form—instead of as a tract, it took on the color of the people and the times. Steeped in the heritage of the people of Appalachia, validating their

experience, responsive to their cries and supportive of their
aspirations and hopes, it was also deeply biblical and kerygmatic. The letter was a sign that—to use the bishops' own
words—the church can be:

> —a center of the Spirit,
> —a place where poetry dares to speak,
> —where the song reigns unchallenged,
> —where art flourishes,
> —where nature is welcome,
> —where little people and little needs come first,
> —where justice speaks loudly,
> —where in a wilderness of idolatrous destruction the great
>   voice of God still cries out for life.

Such a letter encouraged me to believe that our evangelism can be renewed. Something is happening in the land.
Encouraged by a new vision of the kingdom—which they
see as central to the gospel—some Christians are once again
daring to hope. For so long we had banished hope to the far
future or to an extraterrestrial realm. We've shown ourselves
as Christians to be no different in this respect from other
Americans.

The world-view of narcissistic America, Christopher
Lasch says, is "the world-view of the resigned." But in statements like these of Youngstown and Appalachia, and in the
sacrificial action which they point to, I see a sign: people are
no longer willing to be resigned. Their numbers are not
many; but these people of faith have begun to dream again,
to have hope. As a result their evangelism is no longer a
palliative, a soporific, but a challenge, an encouragement.

One final example. An ecumenical Dutch team which
calls itself Oudezijds 100, after its street address in inner-city
Amsterdam, believes, that, in evangelism, it is called to

"double solidarity." It is called to be in solidarity with Christ, to be one with him, as he was with God. At the same time it is called to be in solidarity with the world, following Christ's example and taking up the form of a servant (Philippians 2:7).

The Oudezijds 100 team has for a decade or more lived in what many would call a "God-forsaken" place, where prostitution, pornography, and rank commercial exploitation of human beings—Dutch as well as North African—goes on visibly before your eyes. Oudezijds 100's motto is "Clarity in Freedom." We have, they say, a responsibility to proclaim the Word, and we must do it clearly, respecting the freedom of those with whom we would share it, refusing to compel or manipulate them. They try to live out their lives simply and forthrightly—being of service, building community, seeking by all means to communicate the Word that brings life.

> In Oudezijds 100 we are constantly accused of being activists. Probably correctly. On the other side, with equal force, we are accused of praying too much and doing too little. Probably also correctly. We remain in the quest for the third way.[18]

That third way has led the team into deep and sacrificial engagement in the lives of God's poor—an involvement which, they stress, they can only maintain through deep prayer and immersion in the Scriptures. They are so little understood—either by those who take the first way of otherworldly withdrawal, or by those who take the second way, of "secular activism." But they are sometimes understood by the poor amongst whom they live. Their lifestyle is a witness that communicates the reality of the kingdom in an idolatrous and violent world.

What does this tell us about a kingdom-oriented evangelism? Perhaps—at the risk of oversimplification—we can summarize it in three verbs: we proclaim, we interpret, we summon.

We proclaim what God is about. We announce the coming of the kingdom, its warfare against the reign of evil, the liberation of God's bound creatures.

We interpret how that warfare is going on in our societies. We help people see and name the demonic forces which subvert God's creation. We show them how the Spirit is delegitimizing these powers and loosening their hold on God's people.

As people come to faith, *we summon* them into the kingdom community. This is a community which works for human liberation. At times it is dispersed among others, at times it is engaged in its own action. In both cases it resists the power of death and calls people into life. These are three elements of an evangelism oriented to the kingdom of God.

The man we meet among the tombs of our society is possessed by so many unclean spirits that his name is Legion. These spirits drive him so incessantly that he can no longer be controlled. No social or cultural force is strong enough to master him. So daily, among the tombs and on the hillsides, he cries aloud and cuts himself with stones. When the Lord comes to him he prays, "Lord, do not torment me!" But the Lord casts out the spirits which possess him. Those who come to see the man find him clothed and in his right mind.

Is this perhaps a parable of evangelization in contemporary Western society? If it is, then we can expect to see something else happen as a result.

And as he was getting into the boat, the man who had been possessed with demons begged him that he might be with him. But he refused, and said to him, "Go home to your friends, and tell them how much the Lord has done for you, and how he has had mercy on you." And he went away and began to proclaim in the Decapolis how much Jesus had done for him; and all men marveled.

Mark 5:18-20

CHAPTER 2

The Seventies: New Understandings of Evangelism and an Unfinished Agenda

How did we get to where we are? What has been happening in evangelism around the world? What is the significance of the emergence of a kingdom-oriented evangelism? Let's begin to answer those questions by looking back to the seventies.

The seventies were important years in the history of evangelism in the church around the world, positive, critical years, but not fully decisive ones. At the end of the decade many important questions had been raised but few settled. How the church will answer those questions is the crucial agenda for the eighties. It will determine whether a kingdom-oriented evangelism will be the evangelism of the eighties and beyond.

To realize how far we moved in the seventies, it is only necessary to recall how things stood as the decade began. It was on March 4, 1970, that the Frankfurt Declaration on the Fundamental Crisis in Christian Mission was issued. (See Appendix 1.) The "primary tasks" of mission had been "displaced," the motives and goals of mission had been "insidiously falsified" by the ecumenical movement, it was charged. The Bible had been "surrendered" as the "primary frame of reference" in favor of "a one-sided outreach of missionary interest toward man and his society." The uniqueness of Christ and the gospel had been "abandoned" in favor of "a humanitarian principle." The "essential difference" between the church and the world had been obscured. Instead of mission and evangelism, Christian presence and dialogue had been advocated. This, the German theologians charged in the Declaration, led to "syncretism" and to positively "antichristian directions." The churches had been seduced by an "enthusiastic and utopian ideology falsely equating messianic salvation with progress, development, and social change."

A few months later, as I visited New York prior to taking up a newly established position as Consultant on Evangelism for the United Church Board for World Ministries, I visited Professor J. C. Hoekendijk in his office in a garret above Union Theological Seminary. I wanted to gain his insights into the kind of situation I was getting myself into.

The United Church Board, I explained to him, was convinced it was time to put a renewed priority on evangelism. I knew of Hoekendijk's seminal work in the ecumenical movement on the reconceptualization of evangelism in the decades following the war. I had been greatly impressed by his book, *The Church Inside Out.*[1]

In the last years of my time as a missionary doing primary evangelism in Northern Ghana it had seemed to be just the word I needed to hear, it called me from preoccupation with the process of ingathering Chokosi villages—in the people's movement then going on—to asking the important question "why?" Why did God want the Chokosi people to become Christians? What purpose did God have in mind for this vast ingathering? Hoekendijk had been helpful in enabling me to answer this question in eschatological perspective: God was involved in the process of bringing eschatological shalom to humanity. The gospel enabled people to come to understand what God was about and to take part in this historical project.

I explained to this venerable theologian of mission—how naive we sometimes are!—that I had found his book a necessary complement to the writings of his "colleague across the continent," Donald McGavran, at Fuller's School of World Mission and Institute for Church Growth. McGavran, I shared, had also had a great influence on me. (It was only later that I would come to realize how much at enmity with one another these two mentors of mine were. At the Carter Symposium on world mission at Milligan College in Tennessee in 1975[2] the two of them, together with Peter Beyerhaus, the architect of the Frankfurt Declaration, would face one another in ardent debate. I would be there to witness the clash and to have to put together the pieces of my broken synthesis!)

I explained to Hoekendijk my dis-ease as a United Church missionary with my mission board's lack of emphasis on proclaiming the gospel verbally and calling people to discipleship. I was an anachronism—a United Church missionary who was engaged in these tasks. I lamented that so few of our missionaries were doing these things. Under the Board's new executive vice-president, David M. Stowe, an attempt was going to be made to right the imbalance. The Board would engage in proclaiming the gospel with greater intentionality, not ceasing to do the work of education, medicine, development, and community organizing, but seeking to bring out the "evangelistic component" of these ministries. I was to facilitate this process. How did Hoekendijk see my task?

Without a minute's hesitation he reached across his desk

and picked up a mimeographed document. "This," he said, "is the challenge that has been issued, the gauntlet that has been thrown down. This is what we have to address more than anything else. It challenges at its very root everything we have for the last decades been doing." It was a copy of the Frankfurt Declaration.

That was how it seemed to the dean of ecumenical missiologists at the beginning of the decade. The seventies would be the decisive struggle within world Christianity between two armed camps. Hoekendijk was trying to enroll me in his camp. Later McGavran would try to enroll people like me in his and Beyerhaus's camp.

Hoekendijk's attempt failed. At that time in my life, experiences in the church had moved me to feel that much of what the Frankfurt group was saying was very much to the point. It had been discouraging to me, as a missionary doing deputation work, to discover that many of the folks who had been paying my salary in Ghana had grave doubts about the wisdom of trying to persuade people of other faiths to become Christians.

It had been a tremendous shock to my system, when I came back to the States and was assigned to be missionary-in-residence at one of our United Church seminaries, to see how far secular theology had made inroads. I found myself aghast at the "benediction" with which one of the seminarians ended a worship service: "Go, but do not go in peace, for there is no peace, but go to make the peace."

At the seminary I found it almost impossible to function as a member of a teaching team in the senior course in ministry. No one but I seemed to feel it important to get our bearings in ministry by asking first what the New Testament had to say about it. Ministry was understood as "change-agentry." It was simply assumed from the start that change-agents were what ministers were supposed to be.

It was a lonely year. After a semester of fruitless efforts to raise biblical questions in the seminary as a whole, I gave up. I decided to spend my time differently. I would work with those few other souls I could identify who shared my concern for the Bible, for prayer and the devotional life, and for evangelism. I learned of a group, based in the city where the seminary was, called "The Fellowship of Concerned Churchmen." It was a support group of those United Church clergy—and some laity—who were concerned about the denomination's lack of emphasis on biblical faith, preaching, Bible-centered Christian education, and ministry in the congregation. For some—and I include myself—it was not only a support group but a nascent caucus, with specific goals in church politics. We wanted to move our church back to what we considered to be its foundations.

So that's where I was when I visited Professor Hoekendijk. It was a measure of my naivete that I didn't recognize that that was not where he was. He wasn't in the "other camp" either—whatever that was. Hoekendijk was a consistently biblical thinker, and no one could legitimately accuse him of "horizontalism" or having "abandoned the uniqueness of the gospel."

When I came to take up my job in New York (in July 1971) I pursued a strategy similar to the one I had been led to earlier. I sought to identify those persons in our Board and in other denominations who shared a concern for renewed biblical evangelism. I worked with them, hoping we could move our denominations and the National and World Council of Churches back toward the center. In the meantime, even if we couldn't achieve that goal, we could design programs of biblical evangelism alongside the programs the churches were funding. We could appeal for fairness; just as blacks received special funding, so evangelicals (it was then that I began to feel I was one, not because I had moved but because my church, I felt, had) were entitled to have the church fund the kind of programs we were interested in. I was convinced there would be such an outpouring of positive response from the grassroots that the central structures would recognize we were really calling them to the right thing. I further imagined that in time evangelicals would come again to positions of leadership in the central structures. Many people then exercising leadership, I was convinced, were bankrupt. There would have to be a transfer of power.

How far away those years now seem! The Fellowship of Concerned Churchmen died before it even had to reckon with the perception that its name was sexist. The Frankfurt Declaration? Who speaks of it now? Certainly there are lots of groups in the mainline denominations which still try to do the kind of thing the Fellowship of Concerned Churchmen was set up to do—Presbyterians United for Biblical Concern, the Good News movement in Methodism, and even a new group or two in the United Church. Others can name their own examples.

But the battlefield is set up differently nowadays. It's no longer those calling for humanization as the goal of mission versus those calling for evangelism. It's no longer the central structures versus the pew-holders. It's no longer the "liberals" versus the evangelicals. It's an infinitely more complex scene. And it's one in which people are, by and large, talking when they disagree, instead of hurling anathemas at one another Frankfurt style.

What Happened Among U.S. Mainline Protestants?
One of the big changes of 1980 from 1970 was that offices of

evangelism—both in the denominations and in the councils of churches—were renewed or started afresh. My appointment as consultant on evangelism for the United Church Board was one of a number of such appointments different bodies made during the decade. No matter where you look these days you find a department of evangelism—usually tolerably well funded, adequately staffed, and taking the task of evangelism with the utmost seriousness. These offices are turning out reams of materials and organizing hundreds of programs. They're operating fully in the limelight, not as rump caucuses anymore.

A couple of years ago, I served as consultant on evangelism for the Evangelism Working Group of the National Council of Churches—another new child of the seventies. The working group asked me to write a report on what the mainline denominations were doing in evangelism.[3] I sat for six weeks before a two-foot high pile of materials that denominational evangelism secretaries had sent me. Slowly I became aware that there was a definite gestalt to the evangelism which was being carried on. Differences existed to be sure among the ways different groups conceived of and carried out evangelism, but the similarities were even more striking. I set out to do a composite sketch of what the denominations held in common. I found eight characteristics.

First, no one speaks any longer of a merely "implicit" style of evangelism. Common agreement exists that at some point the gospel must be proclaimed verbally. "The churches," American Baptist Jitsuo Morikawa reflected for the National Council of Churches (in its 1976 Policy Statement on Evangelism, see Appendix 8), were "strangely bound by a reluctance to name the name of Jesus as Lord and Savior.... There is a great need to recover the ability to name the name . . . and bear witness to it . . . ."

This has been and is being done in print, through the electronic media, in lay witness missions and festivals of faith, in visitation evangelism, and even—and this is perhaps the test—in the midst of social action and making pronouncements on issues of social justice. Such pronouncements and such action are much more likely to be theologically grounded and explicitly confessional nowadays than not.

Second, all agree that the congregation of believing Christians is the primary means of spreading the good news. Denominational structures do not exist to carry on this responsibility for the congregations but to help them to do it. Though trained or charismatic individual evangelists may have their role to perform, it is an extraordinary role. Normally evangelism is to be done by the people of God in a given place—for several reasons.

For one thing, in the 1970s we came to appreciate the local once more. In 1973 a minister in Cincinnati told me, "I get the distinct impression the United Church believes in a priestly, sacrificial faith. When the church uses the word 'mission,' what it's telling me is 'Send us the money—we'll sacrifice the lambs for you.' Mission is what takes place at the national level. We're not capable of doing mission. All we can do is fund it."

His protest has been heard. There's been a reaffirmation that the local is central; the city, the neighborhood, the congregation is "where it's at." This is part of a nationwide shift in how we appraise the relative importance of different levels of our common life. We no longer see the local as peripheral; it is more likely that the reverse is the case. Denominations find it hard to raise funds for mission at the national level these days because so many people now claim those funds to do mission locally! The same is true in many national social action movements.

For another thing, we have recognized that one of the goals of evangelism is to bring converts into close, supportive fellowships. National denominations cannot provide these. Unless a church is waiting to graft new believers into its life, the seed will have been sown on shallow soil.

A corollary of the statement that congregations are the main agents of evangelism is a recognition that pastors are not. Though they may be skillful in convincing people of the truth of the faith, they ought not to pre-empt the responsibility of the congregation. Pastors should regard equipping the saints for the work of ministry as a high priority. We have seen a significant movement against "elitism" in ministry.

Third, church renewal has to accompany evangelism. In churches which (whatever their origin) are not gathered communities of believers, a strange thing happens when you study the word in preparation for proclaiming it. "Is this what the faith's all about?" people ask, amazed. "Why didn't we hear this before? We've got to be evangelized ourselves!" Furthermore, when such congregations become aware of what the Bible says the church is, they generally recognize that they are a long way from being it. How can they seriously invite people to become part of a church that is cold and formal? Uncommitted to action in the world? Limited to one race or social class? "We've got to be renewed so we become a better model of what the Bible's talking about by 'church,' " people say.

Fourth, gimmickry and high-powered manipulation are not honest. People are placing a high value on authenticity and sensitivity in evangelism. They speak of evangelism as "talking from heart to heart," "one beggar telling another beggar where to find food," "speaking from a position of vulnerability," "being yourself and communicating what you believe in the context of who you are." The churches are not about to look for a mainline Protestant version of the Four Spiritual Laws.

Along with this goes a real suspicion of religious imperialism which tries to hook people on "your doctrine, your church, your faith." A third party is involved in the evangelistic dialogue. The Holy Spirit will speak to the person directly while you are conversing and will lead that person to an authentic response of faith. That response may be different from your own.

Fifth, in "storytelling" the churches have found a new paradigm for what it is we do as we share the gospel with others. We tell the story of the community of faith; of God's dealings with humanity and his chosen people; of Christ's coming, death, and resurrection; of the Holy Spirit and the gift of new life. We find contemporary ways of retelling the message of the church about salvation and repentance. We are not just teaching "Bible truths" or lifeless propositions, or a philosophy of life, but telling a story, something that's happened and is happening and will continue to happen till the new day has fully dawned. We do this in the context of telling our stories, how we have personally and communally experienced God's grace and found new life. Further we ask those to whom we are witnessing to tell us their stories. We want to explore with them how the story might intersect with their stories.

Sixth, none of the foregoing means we have to be so shy that we don't plan for evangelism with intentionality. A spate of manuals has been produced which aim to help a congregation study its community with its different populations, analyze the extent of evangelization, help them decide whom to approach, and guide them to appropriate methods.

A church cannot simply say, "Everything we do is evangelism" or be content to claim, "We're proclaiming the good news to our world." If it does it will avoid hard questions like "Who's hearing the message and who's not?" "Are people being brought into communities of faith as a result of our efforts?" and "How can we communicate better?"

Seventh, evident in the literature and in what I observe is a sense that the church is wider than anyone's denomination. Though one looks in vain for many signs of ecumenical evangelism—remember when "Joint Action for Mission" was the slogan?—one notes a sensitivity to other Christian fellowships. People are being encouraged to "reach the unreached"; the 1978 Gallup Survey of Unchurched Americans[4] was aimed at helping them do this. A good measure of interdenominational borrowing is also evident in the materials. Occasionally a joint program is put together. EVCOM, the interdenominational training program in evangelism and communications, is a good example.

Eighth, there is a common gestalt in understanding how the proclaimed Word, the incarnate Word-in-act, and the life of the fellowship that does the telling and doing form two parts of one large whole. That's what evangelism is. It isn't just the Word or just the deed or even simply the Word and the deed together. Rather it is the Word and the deed spoken and lived out in the life of the community. Evangelism is like a tripod. If any of its three legs is missing, the tripod will fall. The polarization we saw at the beginning of the 1970s between those who said, "We're doing the gospel" and those who said, "We're preaching the gospel" is gone. Now everyone seems to recognize that both must be done. A growing awareness also exists that telling and doing must be grounded in being: the being of the community as a witness to the fact of reconciliation in Christ.

Just a moment, though. I have been writing about evangelism as an increasingly smaller proportion of the American Christian church, the mainline Protestant communions, has come to see it. But I believe I am describing something that applies in many respects to other communions as well—to the evangelicals, the Roman Catholics, and to the churches descended from the Radical Reformation. More and more I see that what one branch of the church is going through has its parallels in the experiences of others.

Developments in the World Christian Community

In this decade major developments have taken place in the world Christian community with regard to evangelism. An amazing convergence has occurred. From different starting-points, different communions came to the end of the seventies with a remarkably common mind about some of the basic parameters of contemporary evangelism.

I return for a moment to my battleground imagery. John Stott, the Anglican who has had such a strong influence on world evangelicalism over the last few decades, started the decade among the embattled. In the record of the Uppsala Assembly of the World Council of Churches (1968), Stott was in the minority, one of the protesters who took exception to the "horizontalism" of the Council's approach to evangelism. By the end of 1977 he had written a major article listing ten "points of convergence" between the World Council of Churches, the Roman Catholic Church, and the evangelical Lausanne Congress on World Evangelization. In that article he asked whether, despite remaining divergences, the three major documents produced during the decade did not contain a sufficient measure of convergence to warrant some form of common witness. (See Appendix 9).[5] From three different statements representing the Christian spectrum—the

report "Confessing Christ Today" from the Nairobi World
Council of Churches' Assembly (1975), the Pope's "Exhortation on Evangelism in the Modern World" (*Evangelii Nuntiandi*), and the Lausanne Covenant (see Appendices 5, 6,
and 3)—Stott drew together these ten common affirmations:

1. The church is sent into the world.
2. The church's mission in the world includes evangelism
   and social action.
3. The content of evangelism is derived from the Bible.
4. The gospel centers on Christ crucified and risen.
5. Salvation is offered to sinners in the gospel through
   Jesus Christ.
6. Conversion is demanded by the gospel.
7. True conversion invariably leads to costly discipleship.
8. The whole church needs to be mobilized and trained
   for evangelism.
9. The church can evangelize only when it's renewed.
10. The power of the Holy Spirit is indispensable to
    evangelism.

Now it certainly is dangerous to write a history of the
world church on the basis of official pronouncements. For
one thing, people may say the same things and understand
them differently. For another, there may be miles between
what people profess and what they live out. I have a hard
time identifying the effect of Lausanne's insistence that "in
issuing the gospel invitation" we have no right "to conceal
the cost of discipleship" when I see the actual evangelism
carried out by organizations many of whose leaders signed
the Lausanne Covenant. It may just take a long time for the
leaders' insights to reach the hustings. Similarly not all those
in the mainline groups whose churches affirmed that we
need a holistic approach in mission, involving the Word as
well as deeds of love and justice, have begun to act on that.

Nevertheless, ideological projections such as these three statements have an important steering role in moving the church from its position at any one time toward its ideal embodiment. Further, they reflect movements which have been taking place within the bodies that make them.

For all these reasons, therefore, they are important signs of the times. We do well to accord them some respect. We may well be skeptical, for example, about the claim by all three bodies that the church's mission includes evangelism and social action. We may wonder what kind of social action and why Stott says evangelism *and* social action rather than calling evangelism a form of social action. Such questions are legitimate. But we have to remember that, at earlier times, these same bodies would not have written about social action in documents on evangelism. Indeed, in some cases strong resistance would have been raised even to speaking positively about social action. Something has happened.

Similarly, we may wonder about the affirmation that true conversion invariably leads to costly discipleship. Do these churches practice that? we might ask. Nevertheless, all three bodies felt compelled to set it forth as a norm, and that is not to be disregarded.

The Anabaptist/Mennonite influence merits mention at this point. I have spent much of the past decade in conferences and congresses with Mennonite thinkers and mission leaders. They have continually protested against cheap grace. They have been skeptical—while being thoroughly biblical—about "numbers schemes," calling instead for discipleship evangelism. They have insisted that the church is the new society called to model the kingdom. All these have been powerful influences, as has their lived example. In addition, many of us who belong to the mainline communions have been so influenced by such arguments that we constitute a "fifth column" within our denominations arguing for Anabaptist perspectives.

And so, for example, when I read a book like *The Challenge of Church Growth*,[6] first in the Missionary Study series published by the Institute of Mennonite Studies, or the Mennonite booklet *Evangelism—Good News or Bad News?*[7] I find a contribution which has already been part of the mix. Indeed, *The Challenge of Church Growth* was a key influence leading me in the mid-seventies away from the church growth ideology, forcing me to raise basic objections to views I had formerly advocated and acted upon.

Some of the learnings about evangelism in the world Christian community, particularly in other countries, remain to be learned by the American churches. These mostly concern the relationship of evangelism to eschatology. In my report for the Evangelism Working Group I noted that few of our denominations had been able to relate evangelism to the kingdom. The greatest single new insight that has come to us about evangelism in the past decade concerns the kingdom. It has come from Latin America, through the praxis of liberation theology and the Basic Christian Communities movement. They have shown us the inescapable relation between evangelism and liberation.

Christians in mission have been concerned with liberation in the past, even in remote past centuries. They even related a certain type of liberation—usually of a personal type—to the work of evangelism. But they operated with an eschatology which consigned all but personal spiritual liberation to a realm they considered to be of passing, secondary importance. Christians in mission have spoken of that final liberation of all creation of which Paul and other New Testament writers speak when they tell of the kingdom (which, as I showed above, Paul calls "the justice of God"), but they

spoke of the final kingdom as a reality not intrinsically related to history. It belongs to a realm beyond history, to a
transcendent order. True, there may be intimations of it in
this world and age—but we should expect to find them in
peoples' spiritual lives or in the life of the church as the new
society. We should not look for them in the world at large or
in the events of ordinary history.

As I pointed out in chapter 1, Christians have from a very
early time come to operate with a metaphysic which distinguishes sharply between the "eternal" and the "temporal,"
the "heavenly" and the "earthly." Only in brief periods of
"enthusiasm" has the Christian community been able to
dream of realizations of the eternal kingdom within time
and space. We used to speak that way, you remember, of
"eternal life," as that expression is used in the Fourth
Gospel. It was something future, to be held out as a carrot
before us. Then people began to realize that the writer of the
fourth Gospel did not share the world-view of Hellenistic society. He really meant to describe the current life of Christ's
followers as eternal life.

Similarly, Latin American theologians and biblical
scholars have shown how we are still influenced by the
metaphysic of Hellenism when we speak of the kingdom.
Our glasses have kept us from accepting what the New
Testament says about the kingdom: that is has entered our
time and space. Not only our Hellenistic glasses are at fault,
however. It's not a coincidence that it's in the interests of the
world's ruling elite that Christians should have a delayed expectation of the kingdom. This makes them docile, law-
abiding citizens who do not make embarrassing demands today. It threatens the status quo immensely when you have
people around who expect and demand that oppressive
situations be changed.

In chapter 4 I shall speak in detail about the herme-
neutical insights of the liberation theologians. Here let it suf-
fice to cite one contemporary expression of how the Latin
American church has related evangelism to liberation. I take
it from the final document of the 1979 conference at Puebla,
Mexico, of the region's Catholic bishops:[8]

> At the very core of an evangelization that seeks the authentic
> realization of the human being are two complementary and
> inseparable elements. The first is liberation from all the forms
> of bondage, from personal sin and social sin, and from
> everything that tears apart the human individual and so-
> ciety.... The second element is liberation for progressive
> growth in being through communion with God and other
> human beings; this reaches its culmination in the perfect com-
> munion of heaven, where God is all in all and weeping forever
> ceases.[9]

In this citation we find the nexus that it is perhaps the pe-
culiar genius of the Roman Catholic tradition to make—
though it often falls short of it. This question connects the
penultimate time, the time in which we now live, with the
ultimate time, time fulfilled. Liberation, the bishops say,

> is gradually being realized in history, in our personal history
> and in that of our peoples. It takes in all the different dimen-
> sions of life: the social, the political, the economic, the
> cultural, and all their interrelationships.

But that is not to reduce salvation or to take away the
uniqueness of the gospel "through all these dimensions."
The bishops write: the "transforming treasure" of the gospel
"must flow," for it has "its own specific and distinctive
contribution to make...." The bishops do not reduce the
uniqueness of the gospel or diminish the need for the

church. The gospel and the church make liberation full. They explain:

> We mutilate liberation in an unpardonable way if we do not achieve liberation from sin and all its seductions and idolatry, and if we do not help to make concrete the liberation that Christ won on the cross. We do the same thing if we forget the crux of liberative evangelization, which is to transform human beings into active subjects of their own individual and communitarian development. And we also do the same thing if we overlook dependence and the forms of bondage that violate basic rights that come from God, the Creator and Father, rather than being bestowed by governments or institutions, however powerful they may be.[10]

The bishops do not "equate earthly progress with Christ's kingdom. But working for the integral liberation of human beings is," they say, "a contribution to the construction of the ultimate and definitive kingdom." I don't feel that the North American church has by and large been able to make these crucial corrections. We're still plagued by an other-worldliness or an individualism. We haven't taken the gospel seriously enough.

The Unfinished Agenda

I now sketch the church's unfinished agenda as the decade of the eighties begins. One of the unresolved questions at the end of the seventies was the meaning of transcendence. The debates between the Hartford Appeal and the Boston Affirmations (see Appendices 4, 7) were our own domestic form of a worldwide discussion. They were the form in which we debated, with some civility, aspects of the questions Peter Beyerhaus and his Frankfurt associates flung down as a gauntlet five years earlier (though I am not sure the Hartford people even knew of Beyerhaus).

In what sense, the question was debated, does the faith deal with nonhistorical or post-historical realities so that we reduce them unpardonably if we interpret them as applying primarily to the intra-historical realm? For example, when we speak of salvation are we speaking of something beyond history, partially realizable within history, or totally historical? What is the relationship between salvation and the various types and degrees of human liberation? Despite all the effort given these questions in the seventies, they remain on the table for the eighties.

Related to this, how do we understand the kingdom? Can we develop a kingdom-oriented evangelism? What will it be like? Will it help overcome the separation between evangelism and discipleship, between evangelism and social action? I hope that the meeting of the Commission on World Mission and Evangelism of the World Council of Churches in Australia will be helpful on this point. The meeting has as its theme, "Thy Kingdom Come."

Third, we have not really begun to debate a question lying beneath many of the other debates: what is the relation of "the people of God"—the church—and God's people in the world? This question was much discussed in the sixties. It will come back again for further consideration in the eighties. If we are to take the secular realm seriously, we have to answer it. The issue is this: in Scripture and in contemporary theology we speak of God's people, of God's children, in two ways—in a limited sense and in a less restricted way. At some times the term seems to be clearly limited to God's particular people, God's adopted children. At others, we do not limit it at all; we mean the whole of creation. Can we legitimately speak, as Jacques Ellul does in a recent article,[12] and say, for example, that when Paul speaks of how creation is "waiting for God's children to be revealed," this does not mean a judgment in which certain of God's children will be damned while others are declared to be God's children? Ellul believes "that *all of creation* is involved. The revelation that the creation is waiting for is that all are God's children." Is this what we want to say? Must we make any qualifications?

It seems to me that the Holy Spirit is saying something to the churches as they engage in action on behalf of justice. It is forcing us to come to appreciate in a new way the wider sense of Scripture when it speaks of God's children, God's people. Many of us are sensing a need to redefine what Scripture means when it speaks of God's people. This is not to deny the particular sense in which the church is the people of God. So we have to go on to ask: what is the special identity of the church *vis à vis* the whole of God's people?

A fourth and related agenda is one which will, I expect, carry us in the opposite direction, from universalism to particularity. That is the question: who are the poor for whom the good news is intended? The church over most of its history has had no difficulty universalizing the category of the poor. Following Matthew's example in the Beatitudes (5:3, cf. Luke 6:20), it has spoken of the "poor" in ways that would include those who are not economically poor.

Many in the seventies felt called to particularize the category of the poor in a more consistent way, to go back to what they see as Jesus' original intention in the Beatitude and apply the term to the economically poor, to the oppressed. They have produced significant evidence, going back to the Yahwist and the Psalms, that the "poor," the "weak," and the "lowly" are the same people Scripture has in mind when it speaks of the "oppressed" and those deprived of justice. Jesus concretely announced good news for the oppressed. The news was that they would receive justice.

The church, many now say, has gone too far toward spiritualizing the concept of poverty in order to make it of universal application. As Gustavo Gutierrez put it at a Theology in the Americas workshop in New York in 1978, "Nowadays everybody is trying to get a certificate of poverty so they can qualify for this blessing!" We've lost the original sense of the Beatitude in focusing on its possible derivative meanings. If we are to be faithful to Jesus' intention, and to what the Spirit is saying to the churches in their missional involvement with the physically poor, then we have to recognize this: the gospel comes first to the actual poor. It is only through them that it is mediated to others.

The Catholic bishops put it this way in the Puebla document, "The poorest sometimes seem to intuit the kingdom in a privileged and forceful way."[13] (This does not mean that they do not need to hear the gospel and experience conversion, it should be noted.) The bishops feel the church is called to take a missional "preference for the poor and a drawing closer to them."[14] "The poor," they have experienced, "challenge the church constantly, summoning it to conversion, and many of the poor incarnate in their lives the evangelical values of solidarity, service, simplicity, and openness to accepting the gift of God."[15] It remains for the church to identify God's love, that toward which they yearn, to show solidarity with the poor in their struggle. Following the movement of God's Spirit, it will take "a preferential option" for the poor, one aimed at their "integral liberation."[16]

It is one thing to say we must also be concerned for the poor. It is another to say we must opt for the poor in preference to others. That upsets people who believe in a "democratic God." They find it hard to believe that God would "take sides." This will become an increasingly painful church agenda in the coming years, bringing much conflict.

Two remaining agenda items concern the church's internal life. The first of these is the question of how the whole church is related to smaller, committed, more intentional church groupings. Traditionally this question has been described as the relation between the *ecclesia* and the *ecclesiola*. This is a question of utmost personal urgency to me as a member of a small Christian community. Up to this point at least I have felt compelled to maintain my links to standard churches and denominations. I recognize "church" in them. But many of my sisters and brothers challenge whether these churches are the church.

It is here where the influence of the Anabaptist renewal has been felt most keenly. In what has been a major questioning of, if not attack upon, Christendom, hundreds of small, face-to-face, supportive communities have sprung up across North America calling themselves churches. They have questioned whether the bodies which have used the word church to describe themselves maintain enough of the marks of the church to qualify for that title. It was one thing when, in the fifties and sixties, the house church movement developed in North America and Europe. Those house churches usually regarded themselves as part of the great church. But when such groups disavow any need to form part of the established churches, when they say they contain within themselves all the marks of the New Testament church, it is an entirely different question. Then they are no longer *ecclesiolae*. They have become *ecclesiae*.

Are we in the midst of a major watershed of church history? Is the small, intentional community which makes radical demands upon its members the wave of the future church? Or is it, as Emilio Castro has suggested, a sign to the standard churches that they must take their peoplehood more seriously? Can standard churches take on the marks of the *ecclesiola* as Dean Kelley seems to suggest they should in his book, *Why the Conservative Churches Are Growing?*[17]

It's not merely a North American problem. What does the phenomenal expansion of Basic Christian Communities in Latin American Catholicism presage for the future of the Latin American church? Will they continue to be part of the great church? Or will they increasingly move, before the end of this decade, toward an assertion of their independence and sufficiency?

A sixth and final agenda concerns the place and function of what has been called leadership in the people of God. In the seventies we have seen the development of non-elitist decision-making in many institutions of society, particularly under the influence of the feminist movement. We have heard calls for "participation," for "an end to patriarchalism." For those making such calls, will it be enough if the recognized leaders of the church come to understand their role in a new way as to be equippers of the saints for ministry and to be facilitators of the life of the community? Or will they insist that leadership in itself is alienating, that the church, if it is to be the church in its fullness, and if it is to rediscover the meaning of peoplehood, must do away with having leaders and search for alternative, more biblical forms of ministry?

Six heavy agendas. More than a full meal for the eighties and beyond. I for one look forward to this time to see what the Spirit will be saying to the churches.

Editor's note: After this chapter was written, two later important statements were produced, one by the World Council of Churches (Melbourne, Australia, May 1980) and another by the "Consultation on World Evangelization" (Pattaya, Thailand, June 1980). See Appendices 10 and 11.

CHAPTER 3

My Experience as an American Missionary
in the Sixties

The French have a proverb that says, *reculer pour mieux sauter*—if you want to be able to jump far, start by going back a few steps so you get a running start. We've begun to do that. We've looked at present-day evangelism by taking a historical look at what happened to evangelism in the seventies. Now I want to go back one step further, to the sixties. I want to look at where we were in the sixties—not in the same historical style I used to describe the seventies, but through an autobiographical sketch.

My reason for going back to the sixties is that a change came about in the seventies to which I didn't refer in chapter 2. The distinction between "home mission" and "foreign missions" moved further toward collapse. The personal history I want to share may give us some insights into why it has moved this direction.

At the Lausanne Congress considerable dissatisfaction was expressed by "missions" specialists who said, "This isn't the conference we need. We need to focus on the task of spreading the faith across cultural barriers. This congress confuses apples and oranges—putting the evangelization of those who've never heard the gospel in the same basket with the re-evangelization of Christianized peoples." To put the two together questioned the self-understanding of many of us. The church had developed two corps of specialists—those with expertise and experience in "foreign missions" and those with skills and learnings in "home mission."

More was threatened than our job security—though that was threatened when many churches merged foreign and domestic boards in the seventies. What was threatened was the very division between "Christendom" and the rest of the world. We had grown used to seeing the world as divided between two parts—one that was within the realm of God's saving history and one that wasn't. The "unfinished task" was to "reach unreached peoples," to "penetrate the regions beyond," to cross the frontier between the "Christian" and "non-Christian" worlds. A certain "saltwater mystique" was attached to the work of foreign mission—only by crossing the seas did you get into "real mission." Mission at home—though legitimate tasks had to be done—was a pale challenge compared to the task to be found overseas. Those of us in the foreign mission boards felt like pioneers compared to those working with peoples who had been evangelized for centuries.

We were aware, of course, that there were people in our own countries who qualified for the name "heathen." But we said that tongue-in-cheek. They were "Christianized heathen" who basically had to be "called back" to the Christian faith. Peoples abroad, on the other hand, had to be "called out of darkness." Those of us working with "unreached peoples" were doing "primary evangelism." Implicit in that phrase was a sense that all other evangelism—including that done in places where a second- or third-generation church was to be found—was secondary at best. When I moved in 1964 from work in Southern Ghana, where missions had been going on since the early 19th century, to Northern Ghana, where mission work had just begun, I sensed an exhilaration many missionaries have known—at last I was at the frontier.

Later I found, much to my surprise, that what I learned in Northern Ghana gave me a perspective that was of great help when I got back to the States. I never expected that. I hadn't wanted to return to the States for good. When family considerations—my son's need for special education—forced us to return, I hoped the return would be temporary. My experience in Ghana would be wasted, I sensed, if I couldn't continue to be involved in foreign mission. I wrote to John V. Taylor, then head of the Church Missionary Society in England. He had been a missionary in Africa. His deep and perceptive writings had impressed and influenced me greatly. I shared my family problems, asking if he knew of a place in Africa where we could get special education for Tommy so we could "remain on the field."

His reply both surprised and disappointed me. "Don't think that what you've learned in Ghana requires that you spend the rest of your life in Africa. Your learnings will stand you in good stead wherever you are."

It was several years before I came to appreciate what Taylor had said. In my encounter with peoples who had never before heard the gospel, something happened to me which helped me understand all of mission in a new way. Very shortly I found people at home to be as interested in having me talk about domestic evangelism as they were in hearing me describe evangelism among the Chokosis. This amazed me. What did I know about evangelism in the United States? I hadn't even lived in the country for almost a decade. I saw myself as a sojourner here, waiting for a chance to do "real mission" again.

It wasn't just that I had seen evangelism in a more fundamental way. I had seen something else. My experiences in
Ghana helped me see myself, my church, and my culture in
a new way. Seeing myself reflected in the eyes of people
very different from myself somehow helped me to know
myself for the first time. I became aware of who I really
was—where I came from, what my presuppositions and
values were. In my eight and a half years in Ghana I learned
as much about modern Western culture as I did about
Chokosi culture.

What I learned has helped me see the "unfinished task"
as God's continuing mission to all his people everywhere. If
we are to move forward in mission I sense we will have to
become more perceptive about that mission, clearer about
its goals, more sensitive to the people we meet, and perhaps
most of all more understanding of who we ourselves are—
people God is still trying to reach.

Let me therefore invite you to take a journey with me, a
journey back to the sixties. Let me invite you to share a
missionary's journey of self-discovery. It may be you'll find
in that missionary one not unlike yourself. Much of what we
studied in college and prep school, I now reflect, was geared
to answer the questions, "What is distinctive about our culture as North Americans and Westerners?" "What made us
the way we are?"

Part of the answer we were given was that, as North
Americans, we lived in a society without an established
church. The United States in its history had separated
church and state. As Westerners we lived in a culture which
(with few exceptions) had outgrown religious wars and in-
quisitions. Lamentable though it was, the story of Galileo
was past history. Despite periodic resurgences of religious ir-
rationality (as in the controversy over evolution) we had

recognized the importance of allowing the free intellect to go untrammeled in its search for truth.

I discovered that the Africans among whom I lived saw the world differently from me. They saw the world as consisting not only of what was visible but of invisible forces as well. They lived in terror of many of them. On people's bodies and in their homes one could see the talismans and amulets which were meant to protect them from these "nonexistent" forces. I laughed over them many times. The genius of "modern, secular man," I believed with Harvey Cox, was that he had been freed from asking irrelevant questions about who might be in the wings or backstage. "Modern man" only focused on the "real" personages, the actors on the stage. He could look at eclipses and know scientifically what they were and not shrink in terror before them. He could approach epidemics in a similarly rational way. Nor did he seek to blame his sicknesses on anything but what really brought them on, the viruses and bacilli. He did not fear the birth of twins, as the Chokosi people did. He knew the two possible causes of the birth of twins and did not need to fear that it indicated an entrance into the human world of supernatural power.

This gave us a tremendous advantage over Africans, I felt. Since we knew what causes things, we could also find out—indeed had found out in many cases—how to cure them. Africans, on the other hand, and many other "primitive" peoples, had to be resigned to them. They didn't believe that change could take place. They had always had to deal with such problems; they always would. They had no sense of "history." As Mircea Eliade put it:

Archaic man tends to set himself in opposition, by every means in his power, to history, regarded as a succession of events that are irreversible, unforeseeable, possessed of autonomous value. He refuses to accept it and to grant it value as such, as history—without, however, always being able to exorcize it; for example, he is powerless against cosmic catastrophes, military disasters, social injustices bound up with the very structure of society, personal misfortunes, and so forth.[1]

"Archaic man" lived, Eliade said, in a cyclical world of "eternal return," having an ontology "uncontaminated by time and becoming."[2]

When I went to work among the Chokosi I knew I had a whole array of specialists and technicians to call in—government departments, missionary doctors and agriculturalists, community development workers, the whole lot. Together with them I carried out my ministry of changing the world, of making it a better place. As Roland Delavignette put it:

> The world must be changed. This has the compulsion of a religious faith, and the white man is its prophet.[3]

I look again at one of the last books I read as a history major in college. It tells me a lot, I discover, about how I was enrolled in this world-changing mission, the burden of those who had a sense of history. The book was Karl Löwith's *Meaning in History*. There, underlined, staring me right in the eyes, are the following words:

> The future is the "true" focus of history.... The vision of an ultimate end, as both *finis* and *telos* ... provides a scheme of progressive order and meaning, a scheme which has been capable of overcoming the ancient fear of fate and fortune.[4]

As "moderns, the heirs of the Christian Occident, searching for a better world," Löwith explains, "we are in the line of prophetic and messianic monotheism." Our Western world has united the Judaeo-Christian tradition with that of the classical world in a powerful synthesis.[5] "The living toward a future *eschaton* and back from it to a new beginning," Löwith writes, "is characteristic only for those who live essentially by hope and expectation—for Jews and Christians. To this extent future and Christianity are indeed synonymous." Löwith contrasts this with the hopeless, cyclic world-view of classical paganism."[6] The modern man, Eliade puts it, "has the freedom to make history by making himself."[7] To read such words in the fifties and sixties made me proud. It confirmed my own sense, first that we were indeed an enlightened people and, second, that Christian faith was part and parcel of modernism.

My missionary training, I realized as I reread these words, went far beyond the six weeks' course I had at Stony Point. I was trained for mission through all my education. True, my seminary course in comparative religion had sought to give me a sympathetic understanding of other world religions (of the "universal" ones, at any rate—we didn't study African traditional religions because they were just "tribal" religions). But what, it seemed to me, we were doing when we studied them was to look for the "modern," "progressive" developments in them.

The only "universal" religion present in Northern Ghana besides Christianity was Islam. The books I read on West African Islam gave me the impression it was far different from "real" Islam. It was a mixture of ill-understood Koranic teachings and "African paganism." "Is your faith really satisfying to you?" I asked the Muslim agriculturalist the government had assigned to work in our town. I fully expected he would say, "Not really," and I could go on to present a "truly modern" faith to him. My effort at evangelism was cut short when he replied, "Yes, it really is." As a good follower of Hendrik Kraemer and the neoorthodox approach to other religions, I knew it could not be, but I decided not to challenge him.

But the Chokosis were mostly what Christians in Ghana called "pagans" (following the missionaries?) and what anthropologists who didn't know better called "animists." I needed to have not even grudging respect for their "primitive" and "tribal" faith, for it was on its way out. The people would either have to become Christians, I was convinced, or Muslims. African religions were unsuited for the modern world.

I was sure Northern Ghana's salvation—in a secular as well as theological sense—lay in its people becoming Christians. West African Islam was "backward," and the North was blessed with Christian missionaries from America, Europe and Southern Ghana who would lead the people to a faith which would enable them to live as modern persons in a secular, progressive, and "desacralized" world.

I also saw myself as a missionary from the "developed" world to the "undeveloped" world. Henry Sumner Maine had taught us Westerners that we came from a "progressive" society. The peoples of Africa and Asia, on the other hand, came from "stationary" ones. In 1861 he wrote:

> It is most difficult for a citizen of Western Europe to bring thoroughly home to himself the truth that the civilisation which surrounds him is a rare exception in the history of the world.... Much the greatest part of mankind has never shown a particle of desire that its civil institutions should be improved.... There has been material civilisation, but, instead of the civilisation expanding the law, the law has limited the civilisation."[8]

Little of what Maine said became part of our consciousness (not all to our welfare, however, since his study of the development of jurisprudence in the Western world is so clear-seeing). But the adjectives "stationary" or "static" and "progressive" did, alas, become part of the stock-in-trade of Westerners' attitudes toward non-Western societies. As a result, we could only see our own social system as the goal toward which the "development" of non-Western societies should be directed. Now we didn't see ourselves as being ethnocentric. We weren't asking that people become Americans or Europeans. We were just asking that they become "modern," that they adopt the "universal" cultural phenomena which had only developed in Western civilization.[9]

Arend van Leeuwen's *Christianity in World History* was a kind of Magna Carta for many of us missionaries in the mid-sixties. Knitting together what he understood as the core of biblical faith with the greatest achievements of its Western technological child, he spread forth a vision. It was of Christians participating with others in "a collective and gigantic effort on the part of mankind as a whole to achieve a world-wide economic democracy, in which the potential sources of welfare are exploited to the maximum degree and used to benefit as much of mankind as possible."[10]

What did I do with my self-understanding? How did I spend my time? Armed with a Bible, a trunkful of books, a bag of medicines, and a box of seeds and seed-dressings, I trekked hither and yon for the greater part of my six and a half years among the Chokosis, preaching the gospel, sharing Western technology and education, and communicating what was indeed my fundamental presupposition: that all of that was part of one big whole.

Somehow I never felt I was being culturally imperialistic.

At every hand I found my missional self-understanding validated, not just by other Westerners but by Africans of all sorts, Christians, Muslims, those of traditional religions. I shuddered to hear the praises, "You white people are our God. You are redeeming us." I shuddered even more to hear Africans' self-deprecation: "We blacks are no good. The black man knows nothing." I resisted, I denied, I corrected. I sought to validate African culture. I criticized my own. But the attitude of many modernized, "progressive" Africans was that all this was beside the point. Africa would have to change. I was doing the right thing, they said. I needn't have any scruples about it.

One of the hallmarks of my ministry was, however, that I distanced myself from the young, often arrogant, Westernized folk. Turning my back on the town, I spent most of my time in the villages and with villagers, who became my closest friends. I earned the derogatory title, "The Chokosi White Man." I researched Chokosi history and folklore, published a dictionary, established a vernacular literacy series, worked with others to translate the Scriptures, and trained village leaders.[11]

What was it about the Westernized young people that turned me off? Was it just a romanticism about the "unspoiled native," the "noble savage"? Perhaps some of that was present—the West has a curious love-hate relationship with the non-Western world. We want to "develop" the rest of humanity, but somehow when others become like us, we don't like what we see. The individualism, the self-centeredness, the pride of these transistor radio-toting, calendar watch-wearing young men, and their obvious uprootedness were a visible reproach to our own way of life.

I somehow imagined we could have modernization without alienation. I thought the problem might lie in the style of the education and politics we had brought to Ghana. We ought to have been more sensitive to preserving an African style as we imported modern things. The imports themselves I rarely questioned. I didn't see any way of approaching the problem in a way that got beyond style.

At any rate, I gave little support to the schools. It seemed to me they were producing a generation which had the best of neither world. I somehow wished we could develop an alternative system of village-based modern education, carried on in the local language, and an alternative system of popular-based democratic government instead of party politics.

I was sure I believed that God is no respecter of persons (Acts 10:34) and that England, the United States, and Canada were no closer to heaven than Ghana. But when I look back upon it, ten years later, I wonder how deeply I believed that. I believed it as it concerns the basic outward manifestations of culture—language, dress, food, housing, art. But did I believe it at the deepest level? I wonder.

I wonder as I remember how I tried to help Kongba, one of our village Christian leaders, to fulfil his vision of starting a store in his village of Garinkuka. Garinkuka was twelve miles from any store at which the people could buy soap or matches or kerosene. Kongba had saved up about a hundred dollars to stock the store. I introduced him to the wholesalers in Yendi, the nearest large town. For three weeks I took him with me on my weekly trip to Yendi. He replenished his items and increased his stock. On the fourth occasion however, he wasn't waiting for me at the roadside. I got out of the car and walked to his house.

"Aren't you going this week?" I asked.

"No, not this week," he replied, his eyes averting my glance.

"How will you replenish your stock? Or do you still have enough?"

"No, it's all gone, but I won't go this week."

I became suspicious. "You've still got the money, haven't you?" (I'd lectured him on the importance of keeping his business capital separate from his other money. Double-entry bookkeeping, I'd learned in college, was the secret of the development of commerce in Europe in the Renaissance.)

He decided to level with me. "My brother got in trouble. He seduced one of the chief's wives. He had to pay a fine."

"And you gave him your store capital to pay it!"

He looked at me, unbelieving, and nodded. I didn't understand his incredulous look. I was crushed. Now he'd never get ahead, I was convinced. I decided to try once more. "You mean you loaned it to him?"

"Loaned it? He's my brother!" (What a strange world I must come from, he thought, where you loan money to a brother!) What a strange world I did indeed come from. It was a world which valued getting ahead and progress, independence and self-respect, thriftiness and rationality. That, we were convinced, lay at the root of our progress and affluence.

In almost every area we were the ones, we were convinced, who had the answers. The Africans were the ones who had the questions. Ten years later I now know our Western answers didn't come from the Bible. For the last few years, I've begun to wonder whether they were answers.

One other thing strikes me as I reflect. Another party also was around during all that decade. Sometimes it was visibly around, but it was always present to us, whether visible or not. This other party came from "our" part of Henry Sumner Maine's world—the "progressive" part. It was, however, we believed, in serious competition with us for the hearts and souls of Africa. We called it "international communism." Our missionary training prepared us to encounter it, prepared us to expose it, and made us see our Christian faith and our belonging to the "free world" as part of one thing. I realize now we not only had a live eschatology, but a strong sense of apocalyptic struggle as well. Nkrumah's Ghana came in those years increasingly to belong to "the Soviet camp." As missionaries and Western change-agents, we believed we had a part to play in the downfall of what we believed to be a dangerous heresy. Though we remained for the most part publicly apolitical, our presence, our snide comments, and our attitudes made it no secret what side we were on. And if the question came up, we could cite chapter and verse to explain why the communist option was not one Ghana should take. (I mention this because it will be important when we reflect in chapter 4 on objectivity in hermeneutics.)

So this is how I reflect on who I was as a Western missionary in Africa in the sixties. But I'd also like to share what I learned in Africa during that decade. I didn't learn very much in my first two years, when I taught in a secondary school and did not speak any African language. Nor did I learn as much in the twenty-two months I was first in Chereponi as I did after the Lord saw fit to strike me down with hepatitis.

Being a Westerner, I was determined not to waste the six weeks I would have to be in bed. So my sickroom became a classroom. Twice each day Kashim, the old Muslim weaver who weaved seemingly endless rolls of traditional cloth behind my house the six and a half years I was in Chereponi, came into my sickroom and taught me all the proverbs and stories he could recall. I carefully wrote down every word. I had time to reflect on the folklore he shared with me. I began to discern the values of Chokosi culture, the people's sense of the major crises that confront human beings, as well as their understanding of human psychology, the meaning of community, and the direction of life.

My sense of the importance of language increased immensely. I began to see how, in the strict sense of the word, translation is nearly impossible. Old Kashim's stories arose out of a world-view, a cosmology, an anthropology, and a sociology uniquely coined over the course of the Chokosis' history. It was the distillation of centuries of their lived experience. Their sense of humor, their sense of tragedy, their frustrations, their patience, their anger, their sense of justice, and their understanding of love and peace appeared before me as an intricately woven tapestry before which I could only stand in awe.

My demand to understand, to hear deeply, to communicate and share the story of God's Son—as it might seem to one coming out of that world—forced me to go on. Relentlessly I continued to penetrate their world. The whole character of my missionary proclamation changed when I got up from my bed. That John V. Taylor had penetrated the world of Africa when he was in Uganda (which he described in his book, *The Primal Vision*)[12] was a source of encouragement to me. That a Placide Tempels had begun to discern a "Bantu philosophy"[13] made me want to find its Chokosi equivalent. That an Evans-Pritchard could come to understand the culture of the Nuer[14] convinced me that, given patience and understanding, I could cross the gulf between my culture and the Chokosis'.

I never produced a major work. I made no great new discoveries. What I did had significance mostly for myself. Perhaps it was of some help also for the growing Chokosi church, which thus found itself freer to develop its own theology and liturgy. But what I learned became in time of most significance for how it helped me understand my own society. As a recently returned Mennonite Central Committee volunteer, Dorothy Friesen, put it when she visited our church in Philadelphia, "You go overseas to learn how to be a missionary in your own country."

I had never quite understood what my mother and father, who were second- and first-generation immigrants, had meant when they lamented that there was no such thing nowadays as "family." I had had difficulty understanding why my mother went to such efforts to invite all the women on our block in to meet new neighbors. She seemed to understand it in a different way from how I did: as a random collection of people who just happened to reside in the same area, who had no necessary relationship to one another. To me "neighborhood" was a geographical term. To her it was a social one.

But I belonged to a different generation. With me modernization had gone one stage farther. The difference between my parents and myself was that they were not as individuated as I. On the community-individual scale they were farther toward "community," I farther toward "individual." (My son is even farther toward "individual" than I—he hardly knows anyone on our block. He seems to question including even first cousins and grandparents on his Christmas and birthday list.)

In Africa, however, I encountered a society still all the way at the "community" end of the scale. Individuals had their own identity, but this was not their primary identity. Where the Westerner says, "I think, therefore I am," Africans say "I participate, therefore I am." I remember the amazement of a Scottish missionary teacher friend when she assigned an essay topic, "The last time I was alone." Several of her students answered, "I don't think I have ever been alone."

This would merely be an interesting case of cultural differences were it not for the fact that the African view of the importance of community for holistic human development is correct. "It is not good for the man to be alone," the Lord said as he looked at the garden. Persons who are alone are not healthy persons.

Meyer Fortes, whose *Web of Kinship Among the Tallensi* was a pioneering piece of anthropological research in Northern Ghana, returned to the Tallensi a generation after his masterpiece. Much had happened. The modern world had made its impact. He saw one thing which—it struck him, and he confirmed it by speaking with others—he had never seen·before. This was the presence of psychotic individuals. In all his time with the Tallensi a generation earlier, he had never seen a psychotic. Psychosis came with modernization.

If Africans are asked to describe what a human being essentially is, they would say, "person-in-community," not "person who may be in community." Not to be in community is to Africans to be less than human. We in the Western world, I came in those years to recognize, have gone a long way toward such dehumanization.

My second learning is one of the things people speak of when they contrast our world-view with that of the Bible. Life in biblical cultures is not made up of discrete fragments—"soul," "body," "spirit," "matter," "humanity," "nature," etc. All of life is a whole. So it is to the African as well, but it was not that way to me. When, as a pastor, I questioned whether converts should participate in religious ceremonies aimed at appeasing the divinities of the land, that was only partly because of biblical faith. I regarded land as a totally secular matter—"matter" without spirit. It was interesting that we never succeeded as a church in bringing peace to two villages—one of which had become a Christian village—which were fighting over land. But then the aboriginal holders of the land sent a message, saying, "If you continue to quarrel, the land will be spoiled" (the spirit of the land will be angry, and the land will lose its fertility). The three-year fight immediately ended. I must also confess that, despite my preaching that God was the Lord of creation, I spent much time distributing seed dressings and arranging for the sale of fertilizers which contributed to the pollution of that creation. I had not yet learned what Barry Commoner and Rachel Carson have helped to teach the American public, that "everything is connected to everything else."

Another thing I learned in Africa is that the Bible is not the Western world's book. I saw how selective our reading of it has been. We selectively hear and selectively fail to hear what the message says. How often Africans, reading the word for the first time, asked me (or caused me to ask), "Why has your world not followed this teaching of the Lord?" The Bible, I came to see, stands between us. We each hear parts of it that the other cannot or will not hear. Only with the help of people from another world can any of us hear much more than confirms our prejudices. "You'll never understand the Gospel of John," an Indian Christian told a group of us at a luncheon at the Interchurch Center in New York. "You don't understand what it means to be born of the Spirit." We sat there eating our submarine sandwiches listening to him help us understand it. His lunch remained in front of him, uneaten. There were more important matters for him to deal with.

A fourth thing was not a learning but a suspicion. I began to suspect that my Western Aristotelian categories for describing the "nature" of things falsified reality. We Westerners divide between an object's "essence" and its "attributes" or "accidents." Similarly with the gospel, in those years of biblical theology we distinguished between the "essence," or "core" of the message, an unchanging center, and its "accidents," peculiarities due to local culture. To use another, clearer example, we spoke of "unclothing" the gospel of its "cultural clothing" and "reclothing" it in a receptor culture's forms. This model made us feel that we could guard "the essential faith" from change, while making it "relevant" to the needs of people of different cultures. It was a matter of "application" of "basic truths," not changing the message. We "indigenized" the message.

I began to be suspicious of this approach before leaving Ghana. But it was only when I heard the Theological Education Fund begin to speak in the seventies of "contextualizing the gospel" that I was able to express intelligently what I had begun to feel. Something new happened when the Chokosis heard the gospel in the context of their ongoing history. I came to recognize that something original happened which had never taken place before.

Chokosi Christianity in many ways, of course, has parallels with Christianity among other ethnic groups. A common basis exists for Chokosi Christians to talk about their Christian experiences with Christians of those other groups. But, just as no one else has ever been Chokosi, so no one else has ever been or will be a Chokosi Christian. The Spirit gave birth to a new baby when Chokosi Christianity was born. The best model we have to talk about that uniqueness is the one I described in chapter 2—the storytelling model. It may be true that "We've a story to tell to the nations," but we become religious imperialists when we insist that *our* story will turn *their* hearts to the light. We are witnesses to what *we* have seen and heard. It's enough to be witnesses. We are not authoritative interpreters.

All this reflects on our previous discussion about the difference between cross-cultural mission and evangelism at home. Now doubtless there's something to the distinction. But I wouldn't be inclined to make much of a point of it anymore. For one thing, as I shall shortly describe, the Western world where we evangelize has become highly dechristianized. For another, even if we're working with nominal Christians, if we think all we're doing is reevangelizing, we'll not do any new contextualization. We'll assume that what communicated to the parents of the present generation will communicate to their children as well. The children, however, live in an entirely different world from their parents. It's an entirely different world from that in which they themselves attended Sunday school a generation ago. Their encounter with Christ will similarly be a new one today.

A sixth learning. I spent all of my years in Ghana operating under the twin mandate of "evangelization and development." I grew so attached to the concept of development that I resisted heartily when Latin American theologians began to pillory "developmentalism" in the seventies. I felt the concept had served us well. I experienced, however, that at a certain time of the year, as soon as the crops were taken in, almost all the boys and young men migrated to the cocoa farms of Southern Ghana for cash work. Our literacy classes were disrupted, our leadership training programs interrupted, village development projects deprived of needed workers. And all for what turned out to be, after two to six months, a pittance. The young men could be expected to come home with no more than $20.00 to $100.00 to show for all their time away, for all the family disruptions.

Migratory work was a de-developmental factor. But the government of Ghana needed foreign exchange. So it could do nothing to hinder the cocoa economy which almost alone seemed to provide such exchange. Rural life in Ghana will never prosper—and I mean the whole of rural life—until the country is liberated from dependence on cash-cropping, until Ghana develops agricultural self-sufficiency.

After leaving Ghana I came to recognize that the very model of "development" is based on an Aristotelian view of "nature." What takes place in "development"? We develop toward the fulfillment of our potential, our "nature." Our potential is given, already determined before the process begins. We in the West led Africans to believe that to become developed they had to follow the path other peoples— their "elder siblings"—had taken before them. They had to become like us.

Four generations of Ghanaians had bought that model before I went to Ghana. It was only during the years that I was there that alternatives became possible which Westerners could not disqualify by calling them "nativist." The Tanzanian experiment in "African socialism" or "Ujama" has been the chief among them. Here was a form of lived-out contextualization, an attempt, for all its faults, to make use of technology and modern forms of organization without surrendering to them.

I came back to the United States a very different person from the one who had gone out eight and a half years earlier. I found a country which had also changed a great deal. W. A. Visser't Hooft, the former General Secretary of the World Council of Churches, has for many years cau-

tioned the churches in the West against claiming that the
West has transcended pagan ways. In an article entitled
"Evangelism in the Neo-Pagan Situation"[15] Visser't Hooft
exclaimed several years ago, "It is high time that Christians
realize that they are confronted with a new paganism."

I have difficulty using the adjective "pagan" to speak of
African traditional religions. In Latin a *paganus* is simply a
peasant, a person who lives in the country. Pagan religion in
the late Roman Empire was simply that religion which was
practiced by people who were not urban sophisticates. In the
rural areas Hellenistic religion died hard. In one sense it is
accurate to use the adjective "pagan" to describe African religions; they are religions of the countryside, religions connected with agriculture and fertility, with planting, reaping,
and harvest. (They are, of course, much more.) But only if
we are linguistic purists can we speak of these religions as
"pagan" without causing offense. For "pagan" has come to
mean "heathen, one who has no religion." It was a term
used to describe those in the Mediterranean basin who were
neither Jews, Christians, nor Muslims. Hence, it has come
to be a negative definition, a non-definition.

What Visser't Hooft means by it is something else. It is
paganism, he says, to offer reverence and worship to created
things instead of to the Creator (Romans 1:25). Pagan religion is to him a form of nature religion, "immanentist, inclined to pantheism, relativistic, romantic, individualistic"
(Troeltsch). Friedrich Nietzsche was to Visser't Hooft the
"most influential of the prophets of paganism." He upheld
the cause of Dionysus against the Crucified. Visser't Hooft
declares:

> What has happened in our time, is that this religion of the in-
> tellectuals has ceased to be esoteric and has touched a very

considerable part of humanity.... The film, the paperback
and the modern theatre present the new religiosity to all who
have ears to hear and eyes to see. The message is that life itself
is divine and that the time has come to get rid of the life-deny-
ing doctrines and morals of the Christian faith.[16]

Visser't Hooft appealed to the churches to appoint modern
evangelists to make a deep study of the new paganism,
much as we study Hinduism or Buddhism. We should take
great pains to explain the Christian faith in terms which are
meaningful to those who have turned away from it in favor
of a form of nature worship.

It was indeed a surprise to me, upon my return to the
States in 1970, to see large sections of bookstores devoted to
the occult. I had been used to seeing obscure occult
bookshops in New York as I grew up. To find such books in
the general shops amazed me, however. I saw that many
were about witchcraft. "These must be a put-on," I reasoned. "In a secular society such as ours no one would take
this seriously!" Studying their contents, I received a shock.
The authors were quite serious.

I thought I had left witchcraft behind when I left Ghana!
But here were books which told you how to make potions to
triumph over your enemies, have success in your work, and
be able to seduce the person of your choice.

Incredulous, I asked the bookstore manager, "These
books can't be serious, can they?"

"I wish they weren't," he replied, shaking his head. "I get
nervous every time I sell one."

I discovered that people were also into astrology in a way
I had never seen before. One evening I came into my office
and found my secretary hard at work retyping a dog-eared
computer horoscope he had had done several months

before. It was his everyday companion. As I did deputation work, I found, in the homes of pastors and good church people, books on astrology, signs of the zodiac, specially imprinted T-shirts, all sorts of astrological paraphernalia. "What are you?" people asked me. But I thought astrology had been as discredited as phrenology! It has no scientific basis whatsoever. So I took my son to the planetarium to see a show on the signs of the zodiac, I expected that an institution devoted to science would clearly demonstrate the absurdity of astrology. But I was amazed to see that it did not challenge astrological beliefs at all.

Here was a paradoxical situation. Though the seminary at which I taught was deeply into secular theology, "secular man" was into nature religion! Some Christians, however, were also into a reappraisal of natural religions. "Every religion," the former college chaplain who had first introduced me to the faith a decade and a half earlier, said "diabolizes its predecessor. It overstates the case against it. We have to reappropriate what's good in those earlier approaches." He had become a Jungian analyst, and he counseled with people about their dreams and the archetypes which appeared in them. He and his wife made personal use of the I-Ching, and they said they found it as useful as prayer.

Several theologians were into native American religion. Responding to nascent feminism, some were seeking to "correct" the patriarchalism of biblical religion through the addition of other than Christian perspectives. Those heavily involved in ecological concerns similarly felt that the Judaeo-Christian tradition involved too great an objectification of the created order. They sought a theology which would call humankind to relate to God through nature rather than to dominate the natural world.

The claim of the biblical theology movement that Christian faith was a form of radical monotheism was being challenged on every side. The "principalities and powers, the real existence of which I had come to believe in while in Ghana, were alive and well in Middle America. I remembered what a Dutch missionary friend in Ghana had said to an African who asked him whether paganism existed in Europe. "It's been submerged for many centuries," he said, "held in check by the strength of the church, but those powers are still there. When they see an opportunity, they come to the surface again." But I knew he wasn't thinking only of Diana, Osiris, or obscure forms of witchcraft. He had had a horrible experience of Nazism. When he spoke of pagan powers, he didn't mean only individualistic forms of nature religion. He was referring to world-historical powers which had as their goal the defeat of God's rule on earth.

That friend's comment provided a bridge for me as I sought to get my bearings in the States again. Perhaps I had not left the "mission field" after all. The missional task embraced both worlds. Just as my task in Ghana was to proclaim the sovereignty of God, so that task had to be performed in the United States as well. In both worlds there were other candidates for sovereignty, powers which sought to become supreme in human life, which challenged the lordship of God.

In chapters 5 and 6 I will go into this matter in greater depth and show how I was led to go beyond "neopaganism" to an awareness of the ultimate challenge to God's rule: the principalities and powers. I will explain how I came to see evangelism as an activity closely related to exorcism.

But before I can come to that, I must explain how I learned to interpret the Bible in a radically different way.

CHAPTER 4

Toward a New Interpretation of Biblical Evangelism

I don't know how many conferences I've been at where the first topic listed is "The Biblical Basis of Evangelism" or "The Biblical Basis of Social Action" or something like that. I've spoken at such conferences. I've even designed them! But I've come to have grave doubts that we do either the Bible or the topic under consideration any favor by saying the "biblical basis" comes first and concrete consideration of the task follows after. I've now become convinced that, if our evangelism is to be renewed, we need to develop a new understanding of how to read the Bible. We need to be more conscious of our hermeneutic, our way of interpreting Scripture.

As I described in chapter 3, I was reading a lot into Scripture in my missionary work in Ghana, but I was unaware of it. I thought I was simply doing "biblical evangelism." But I was doing a lot more—or less—than that. Now many people would conclude what I needed to do and what the church needs if this analysis applies to others is simply to become more aware of our lack of objectivity. We need to distance ourselves from our nonbiblical presuppositions and be more rigorously biblical. We should develop more "inductive" methods of Bible study. Those who say this don't question our received model of how to read and interpret the Scriptures. It is, however, a comparatively recent model, based in the Biblical Theology movement of the postwar decades.

The Biblical Theology movement, as I was trained in it at the end of the fifties, seems to have had six presuppositions:

1. You begin by considering the texts.
2. In order to be sure that you can read them objectively, you divest yourself of who you are, your place in the church, whatever ideology or world-view you hold, and your previous understanding of what Scripture says. While you are doing this you must suspend all evaluative judgments.
3. You look in the various texts for what they are affirming in common. Your expectation is that you will be able to emerge with a piece of "biblical theology"—"the biblical view of man," "a biblical theology of justice," "the biblical nature of evangelism," or whatever.
4. You then apply what you have learned to specific current situations and to the life of the church. °

°The assumption is that it is situations which change, but the Bible remains the same. It's like one of the verses in a German folk song,

> In Breman, at the station,
> There's really something to see:
> All the trains go on to other places,
> But the station stays right there!

Our assumption is that the basic teachings of the Bible are like that station; they never move, but situations and contexts change. Though we find in the Bible texts which demonstrate a distinct historical, situation-specific coinage, we divest them of that. We uncover the "timeless, ahistorical essence" of biblical teaching. Why do we do this? Because we want an absolute rock of certainty. We think we need this in order to have a biblical basis for action today. (In actual fact we also "dehistoricize" *contemporary* situations, removing their cultural specificity, so that we can relate them to the "dehistoriziced" Scripture teachings with which we operate.)

   5. If different communions and parties in the church can all
      follow this approach, we will find the way to unity.
   6. Although we believe that the Holy Spirit is alive and active
      today, the Spirit is active in doing what the Spirit has al-
      ways done in all times and places. God will not reveal new
      truths to us today, but only new applications of eternal
      truth.°

The Biblical Theology movement was not, it's important
to recognize, a unique movement. It was simply the application to theology and the Scriptures of the general academic
approach common to all Western scholarship. It prides itself
on its "objectivity," its "presuppositionlessness," its "value-
neutrality." It is an expression of faith in a technology of
scientific study.

Biblical Theology made real contributions to the history
of the church. In the course of biblical study many discoveries were made. Many useful tools of analysis were
developed. Christian scholarship developed a catholicity
which has brought us, at least as denominations, much closer
together.

But as I survey the scene today, it seems we have come to
a series of impasses which Biblical Theology can't help us
overcome. Some of them have been caused by Biblical
Theology itself. Biblical Theology stands in the way of our
dealing successfully with agendas like those I listed at the
end of Chapter 2: developing a kingdom-oriented evangelism, understanding the relation between the people of God
and the world, understanding what good news to the poor

°This is a latter-day reflection of the position which the Western church
took in the *filioque* controversy, when it added the phrase "and the Son"
to the Nicene Creed's confession that "the Holy Spirit proceeds from the
Father." The Spirit is subordinate to the Son.

means, resolving the question of history and transcendence, and so on.

It seems that another way of reading the Scriptures, another hermeneutic, has far more promise of helping us move beyond the impasses. I find that approach in our new understandings of contextualization, in my former teacher Brevard Childs' introduction of "canon criticism," in the writings of Walter Wink and Juan-Luis Segundo, in the reflections on evangelism of Walter Hollenweger, in some black and feminist theology, in the writings of John V. Taylor, and elsewhere.

In this hermeneutic the first thing we have to assume is that we are who we are. We cannot divest ourselves of our personality, our culture, and our ideological perspectives. It's a mistake to hope that we can attain an Olympian posture of objectivity. We have interests; we exist in society; we are partisan, whether we recognize it consciously or not. We cannot pretend to be neutral or universal, like Melchizedek, "without father or mother." Kongba helped me recognize this when we discussed how he had used his store capital to help his brother pay his fine. My Chokosi Bible students helped me recognize this when they asked why my culture didn't hear certain teachings of Jesus. The Muslim agriculturalist helped me see this when he told me his faith, "medieval" though it seemed to me, was personally satisfying to him (see chapter 3).

"The value-neutral, ahistorical point of view is an illusion," Walter Wink writes. We all look at Scripture from the point of view of definite metaphysical, ontological, and empirical judgments. Our faith in reason, our belief in progress, our "ontology of naive realism"—in which we see modern times as the apex of human history—all of these give us away. When we study Scripture we are not doing "purely empirical, deductive research."[1] As John Howard Yoder puts it, we not only consider the faith of the writer we are studying and the writer's witnessing purpose, but as interpreters we ourselves read the texts from a position of faith.[2] What he says about faith applies to our social perspective and our class or sex interests. We do not operate without presuppositions.

An amusing incident took place at the Puebla conference. Points of view were presented which angered some of the more socially conservative prelates. They charged the progressives with bringing ideology into the discussion. "Let him who is without ideology cast the first stone," Bishop Schmitz, a Peruvian, responded.[3]

Being aware of our distinct perspective enables us to begin to seek a different kind of objectivity. This is not an "objectivism" in which we presume to be what we cannot. It is rather a position in which we are critically aware of ourselves. Instead of excluding evaluations, we make them, aware that we are doing so.[4] But we are "pervasively suspicious" about our ideas and value-judgments.[5]

This type of suspicion about ourselves frees us to read the Scriptures in a liberating way. We accept our own specificity. We recognize further that what we have in the Bible is a collection of equally specific, historical witnesses. Indeed, there are no other type of witnesses. Every encounter between God and human beings recorded in Scripture was a specific encounter. It took place in a given, often discernible context. Over a period of twenty centuries many different faith encounters took place.[6] What is the Bible, then? It is not a timeless revelation which leaves the onus on us to see how it might be applied. It is a collection of concrete, historical examples of how different persons heard God speaking and how they understood and acted on it.

"Western philosophy usually proceeds by trying to generalize," John Howard Yoder writes. The Bible, however, isn't interested in this kind of truth, Yoder says, "but only in those things which truly were done in a particular time and place by a particular divine initiative."[7] We value the particularity of God's revelation. We don't feel we have to dehistoricize or demythologize it. Nor do we, at the other extreme, have to make it an absolute (retreating into an irrelevant archaism, in which we present the world of Eunice and Lois, the world of David and Absalom, the world of Galatia and Pisidia as the "real" world, expecting people today to live emotionally in that world in order to experience God's revelation). Nor do we have to choose among the texts those which we find relevant for our own use, and form a kind of "canon within the canon" of preaching texts we use.

"By taking seriously the canon," Brevard Childs writes, we confess along with the church through the ages "the unique function that these writings have had in its life and faith as sacred Scripture." Each new generation then seeks to work out its own faithfulness to God by searching the Scriptures for renewed illumination. We don't reject biblical critical methods. We "exploit to the fullest the best tools available." Using these methods and understanding our task as a new one, we approach the canon. "In joyful wonder and even surprise," we see the Scripture become the bread of life yet again.[8]

This involves a recognition that a distance exists between the worlds in which the Scriptures were written and our world. We live in a new historical moment. By disciplined theological reflection we analyze the issues which were at stake in biblical encounters and we discern those encounters which are most closely related to us.[9] We will not ever, at

any one time, find God speaking to us through all the encounters equally. The liberation theologians, for example,
have been struck by the Exodus texts. There they find a link
between God the liberator and the political process of liberation. "In no other portion of Scripture," Segundo writes,
"does God reveal himself in such close connection with the
political plane of human existence. Segundo finds it
perfectly legitimate for the liberation theologians to
concentrate on these texts and seek to extract their full
meaning. But that does not mean they must make the claim
that all Scripture says the same thing! He finds their attempt
to see a close connection between Jesus and the Zealots a bit
"forced."[10]

You can begin to sense what is happening with this new
approach. We do not attempt to reinterpret the whole of the
Scripture on the basis of some preferential texts. When we
do that, they become, because of our sense of empathy with
them, a canon-within-the-canon for us (as, for example,
Luke 4:18-19 has become that for us in this decade and as
Romans 3:21-26 was the text a decade earlier). Rather, we
take the diversity of Scripture exactly as it is. We do not
force any "whole" interpretations.

Segundo helped me recognize how I made John 10:10, "I
am come that they might have life, and that they might
have it more abundantly," into a basic divining rod for my
work in Northern Ghana. The text, as I interpreted it, justified everything that an optimistic, world-changing
missionary wanted to do! I conveniently overlooked the
distance between my melioristic world outlook and that of
the Fourth Gospel. John 10:10 became a warrant for interpreting all of Scripture with postmillennial enthusiasm. It
was a wonderful ideological buttress for a theology of
development.

We do well to be suspicious of whatever ideology seems to come to us too easily. If we're reading Scripture authentically, it becomes something that stands over against us; we feel a resistance in it, a tension, an opposition. We have to recognize that we have an innate tendency, as human beings, not to want to be unsettled.[11] We resist anything which causes us to experience what the anthropologists call "cognitive dissonance." We prefer to have our systems, like our milk, homogenized. But if they are too homogenized and if we're "too much at ease in Zion," the chances are we're not reading sacred Scripture.

For when biblical evangelism is really happening in the church it's a terribly unsettling thing. In the story of Peter and Cornelius in Acts 10 Walter Hollenweger finds a paradigm of what happens when the evangelist really reaches across frontiers in response to God's unmistakable summons. The journey leads through almost invincible self-doubt to inevitable quarrels. "The real evangelist," Hollenweger writes, "is by the nature of his calling something of a heretic. He never knows beforehand how his message 'comes alive' in the hearers' context." It may lead him or her to do things they never dreamed of—dangerous, forbidden, heretical things like entering the homes of Gentiles, eating with them, and baptizing them without a confession of the Trinity (and without a period of catechization!)[12]

It's not only our fellow church members that we may offend. We ourselves may be scandalized. In pursuing biblical evangelism we take the risk that our hearers will correct our understanding of Christ. When old Kashim helped me translate the Scriptures, he absolutely confounded me by stubbornly refusing to agree with my translation of 1 Corinthians 15:28: "Then God will be all in all." The best Chokosi expression of God's full reigning glory was to say that God would "exercise kingship over everything," I explained to him that we needed a way of expressing God's complete coronation over creation. The old Muslim thought about it and said that would work, but my translation wasn't acceptable as was. "And God *the King* will exercise kingship over everything," he corrected.

"But the words, 'the King' aren't in the text," I told him. But it was hopeless. It was impossible for him to conceive of any situation in which God was not already King. Kashim made me worry whether I too easily accepted the secularity of the world.

Something was harder for me to accept than Kashim's caveat. That was the desire of the Chokosis to affirm an ongoing relationship under God with their ancestors. To my culture the dead are simply that, the dead. To the African, as John Mbiti has pointed out, they are the "living dead." Yet every attempt by African Christians to affirm the living reality of departed ancestors scandalizes Western Protestant missionaries. We have had such clear (polemical) training against praying for the dead that we resist this strongly. Are we, I wonder, resisting God's Word to us concerning our own relationship with previous generations? Or is it, as I thought at the time, merely a "hang-up" of Africans?

One thing more. I had learned in seminary that Jesus Christ is unique and that God's self-revelation comes to us as "a bolt out of the blue." I was suspicious of all "natural theology." I did not expect to learn about the God and Father of our Lord Jesus Christ from followers of other faiths. I could only be on the giving end of any dialogue with Muslims and traditional religionists, I was convinced. (This fit well our Western sense that we could only be on the giving end in technological and social change also.) It was something of a defeat, therefore, for me to come to the point of having to admit that my dialogue with many Muslims and followers of Chokosi religion had led me to a different conclusion. I came to believe they worshiped the same God I did, even though they did not know God's incarnation in Jesus. I had no doubt but that they could, and did, learn much of God through hearing the gospel. I didn't see it as a matter of indifference whether they would confess faith in Christ or not. (I have still not become a universalist!) But I had to rewrite a substantial portion of my basic theology to affirm what these people taught me.

Now let me draw the parallel. I sense that much of the middle-class Western church is in the same position today as I was then concerning another aspect of God's self-revelation: God's self-revelation to the poor and unjustly treated.

God communicates directly to them. They know that God sides with them. They do not gain this knowledge from us as the result of Christian mission. We find it among them. How do we deal with this? It upsets our understanding of how God communicates—without us as intermediaries! It upsets our notion of God's "democratic ways"—is God really one who takes sides? Could we possibly be on the wrong side? By being powerful and affluent have we become deprived of God's blessing? Have the poor gained God's blessing just by being poor?

This would have tremendous missional consequences. It might mean our whole style of mission would have to be changed. The Catholic Church has made great strides toward making such a change. They have been proclaiming that God has taken a "preferential option for the poor." Whether it be in the work of Mother Teresa or in the speeches of Pope John Paul II or in the documents from Puebla, Catholicism has been willing to take this risk.

Kenneth Cragg, one of the most perceptive of our Christians in contact with the world of Islam, tells us something we would never expect about Palestinian Arabs. In the last few years, out of their uprootedness, out of their unjust suffering, they have experienced a strange sense of coronation, he reports, with a crown of thorns such as Jesus wore. Though they have not studied the New Testament in detail, the crown of thorns has become an important symbol in their literature and art and everyday expression.

You can read every text about the poor in the New Testament, I suppose, and demonstrate on historical exegetical grounds that it's poor followers of Jesus who are intended, or at least poor, God-trusting Jews. You can also, though not with the same degree of success, argue that it is not material poverty in and of itself that is the criterion for God's gracious visitation and promise of salvation. Similarly you can make good arguments, using the examples of Joseph of Arimathea, Barnabas, and others, that it is not the possession of riches as such that makes persons unable to get into the kingdom. If you do all that, your belief structures, your understanding of mission, and your economic systems can remain intact. You can be sure that no radical changes are called for.

But Pope John Paul II, and in many respects Pope Paul VI before him, as well as several synods of bishops and episcopal conferences have chosen not to nuance their words as carefully. "God has taken a preferential option for the poor," the pope declared constantly throughout his trips to Puebla and the United States. The pope made clear that he did not mean that there is a blessedness in poverty, suffering unjustly and unwillingly for its own sake. No, God's preference for the poor means that God is behind efforts to liberate them, to bring about justice. At Puebla the pope declared that even the church's teaching holds that "there is a social mortgage on all private property." Those who own private property have no absolute right to it.[13] If the common good demands it, he said, there is no need to stop at expropriation itself.[14] To the Indians of Oaxaca and Chiapas he even made it clearer than he did to the bishops that the gospel calls the church to be partisan on behalf of the poor, to be in solidarity with the poor in their struggle for dignity and justice.[15]

A close observer of the Catholic Church, Robert McAfee Brown, feels the Spirit blowing in its still halting efforts to reshape its priorities in accordance with what the Spirit has been showing it. He proposes a most un-Presbyterian gauge for telling which of the uneven Puebla statements will be validated:

> Only those statements will have ongoing significance which can be read in the presence of the poorest of the poor and enable all who hear them to begin in a new way to see the world through the eyes of the poor and to make a preferential option to side with them.[16]

The tricky thing here is that such an option will make us cross the frontier. It means we will look for signs of the activity of the Spirit not only in the church, or perhaps not even mostly in the church, but outside. But if we do that, our evangelistic activity will become "a bone of contention."[17] That's "what the good news is by definition," Walter Hollenweger replies, "not just between the Christian and the non-Christian, but between Christian and Christian."[18]

Many people want evangelism to be just "the old, old story, good enough for Peter and good enough for me." But the good news is an event, something new, not just "a repetition of something *déjà vu*.... It demands rethinking and reshaping instant by instant."[19] If that's what the gospel is, it should show up that way in the New Testament. It should be just as fresh and diverse as a collection of different testimonies to God's surprising self-revelation. It shouldn't be all harmonized and smooth, with no rough edges. A contextual gospel will be very different from a propositional one.

When we read the New Testament what do we see? Four gospels, not just one, a James as well as a Paul. Lying behind the documents, able to be discerned by biblical criticism, is one controversy, one bone of contention, after another. That all of these documents have been incorporated into the canon is a confession: a confession that through these writings, diverse as they are, the church believed God had mediated the good news of Jesus to different people.[20] The church had no harmonized version, nor did it expect that God's revelation in its own time would necessarily be less conflict-ridden.

Yet by putting all these writings into a canon the church was nonetheless making a strong affirmation. These writings should be normative for the church throughout its entire future life. Through their faithful reading of the canon, future Christians would be truly guided to discern God's revelation in their places and times of obedience. They would not have to proceed henceforth without road maps, without guidance. They could trust in the Scriptures. They could evaluate their perceptions of God's working in their own times in terms of the congruence of their experiences with the apostolic testimony.

There is something objective about that confession, about that faith, something absolute. There is a difference between a faith like that and an ideology. An ideology, Segundo writes, makes no pretensions about representing any objectively absolute value. A faith does. In faith we have an "en-

counter with an objective font of absolute truth." Now as a
result of that encounter, in an effort to give truth and meaning to our lives, he says, we develop historically particular,
relative ideologies, plans of action, and stratagems. As situations change, these ideologies change. They become dated.
Each time this happens we're forced back to a new encounter with the absolute revelation of our faith. We're
forced back to the gospel message.

But what do we find there? Many of us still hope to find
"answers," prescriptions, and concrete truths for guidance.
But Segundo challenges us. We won't find them there, he
says. God only offers us absolute objective truth through
relative ideologies. That's what we find in Scripture itself.
"Here is what Jesus did *in a given situation, at a specific
time.* Here is what Paul did *when Peter had come to An-
tioch.* Here is what Peter said when *Ananias and Sapphira
had kept back part of the offering.* Here is what Jesus did
when he saw the money-changers in the Temple."[21]

All we have in the Scripture, therefore, are "historical encounters, encounters bound up with relative contexts."

> We rediscover the decisive importance of the (historical)
> density of the Bible. Over a period of twenty centuries dif-
> ferent faith-inspired encounters took place between human
> beings and the objective font of absolute truth. All of these en-
> counters were historical; hence each of them was relative,
> bound up with a specific and changing context. What came to
> be known or recognized in each of these encounters was an
> ideology, but that was not what was learned. Through the
> process people *learned how to learn* with the help of
> ideologies.[22]

Let me pause a moment. Most Americans tend not to use
ideology in the narrow sense in which Segundo does. "In the
news" in the United States Herbert Gans writes,

> ideology is defined as a deliberately thought-out, consistent, integrated, and inflexible set of explicit political values, which is a determinant of political decision. As a result, ideology is deemed significant mainly in communist nations and among parties and adherents of the Left and the Right, both overseas and here. Given that definition, most American political groups are thought not to be ideological; and the news does not accept the possibility that sets of less deliberate or integrated political values are also ideologies.... These are perceived as shades of opinion; and being flexible, they are not ideologies.[23]

It is important that we not lose contact with what Segundo is saying because of our aversion to the use of the word ideology to describe what we ourselves do. By *ideology* he is not referring to full-blown ideological systems, e.g., capitalism or communism, but to highly specific rationales, understandings, stratagems, plans of organization, and proposals for action which we use in working out our response to given (in our case missional) situations. For example, how do we understand what is involved in a given situation? What resources do we as a congregation have at our disposal? What would constitute effective action toward achieving the goals we believe God wants us to achieve here?

Our reading of Scripture inspires us to develop such ideologies, time-bound and relative though they are. Without them we can do nothing. But as we act on them and the world changes, our ideologies must change. This forces us back again and again to the Bible, to ask questions of it, to wrestle with it, and to see things we never saw before.

But what does that have to do with evangelism, you ask? Isn't evangelism telling people about Jesus? I have written and spoken regularly saying just that. The liberal effort to distinguish between the gospel *of* Jesus and a gospel *about*

Jesus, I've written, just won't wash. It is entirely unfaithful
to all the discoveries of historical exegesis to claim that the
church perverted Jesus' message about the kingdom of God
and made it into a message about Jesus instead.

I described in chapter 1 how the good news that is proclaimed is "the good news of the kingdom of God," or "the
good news of the kingdom of heaven" (in Matthew's pious
avoidance of the name of God) or simply "the good news of
the kingdom" (See Matthew 4:23; 9:35; 24:14; Luke 8:1;
16:16). During the Lord's lifetime the disciples as well as the
Lord announced the good news that God's kingdom has
broken into human history.

In Acts, however, written by the same Luke, the evangel
is sometimes "the good news of Jesus Christ" (see 5:42;
8:35; 11:20). In Acts 10:36 it is the "good news of peace by
Jesus Christ." A change has taken place. When the apostles
preach the good news they preach Christ, the one who
himself preached the good news of the kingdom. When the
apostles began to preach Christ, that didn't mean they no
longer preached the kingdom. As Acts 8:12 shows, they announced the "good news about the kingdom of God and the
name of Jesus Christ." They saw Jesus and the kingdom as
intimately connected.

What's the difference between the pre-resurrection and
post-resurrection proclamation? God had, according to Matthew 28:18, given all authority to Jesus. As a result of his
self-emptying and death, God had "highly exalted him and
bestowed on him the name which is above every name, that
at the name of Jesus every knee should bow . . . and every
tongue confess that Jesus Christ is Lord, to the glory of God
the Father." But that hymn, which Paul quotes in Philippians 2:5-11, was used by the church before even the first of
the Synoptic Gospels was written. The Synoptics were writ-

ten by persons who affirmed the centrality of Jesus Christ for Christian faith. It's the firm conclusion of biblical scholarship that the old liberal effort to discern a "pre-Pauline" Jesus before Paul's "corruption" of the message into a message *about* Jesus was an exercise in futility.

The most important thing Christians know about the kingdom is that Christ is the key to it. It was in his coming, in his mission, that the kingdom of God entered human history—a totally new thing, the decisive break between the old age and the new. "Among those born of women," Jesus said, "none is greater than John; yet he who is least in the kingdom of God is greater than he" (Luke 7:28).

How could those who heard and remembered Jesus' teaching about the kingdom cease to preach about it and act and live in consciousness of it, when they came to recognize that Christ's lordship was a central datum of evangelism? They couldn't. If they were to proclaim him as Lord and King, that could only be in the context of their proclamation of the kingdom of which he was King.

But Paul, as is well known, does not generally write about the kingdom of God. Isn't that a problem? No, for although Paul did not tend to write about the kingdom of God directly, using those very words, he wrote about it regularly, translating it, for a Gentile audience, into "the justice of God" *(dikaiosune tou Theou)*. For Paul the justice of God, which we usually translate somewhat archaically, "the righteousness of God" (as in Romans 3:21-26), is not the description of one of God's attributes (as we took it to be at an earlier stage). It is a dynamic concept, an event which has taken place. God has, Paul believes, acted in Christ to establish just relationships between humanity and the Godhead, and among human beings. That is what the kingdom of God is; and this emphasis remained central for Paul.

So it shouldn't surprise us when a late text like Revelation 14:6-7 says the evangel is that all nations should honor God, "for the time has come when God will judge humankind." The good news is that God is ending all injustice and bringing all creatures into right relationships both with God and with each other (the eschatological shalom or peace of which Ephesians speaks, which comes "through Jesus Christ," Ephesians 2:18). So it is unfaithful to the one message of Jesus and the apostles to call people to relationship with Jesus as his disciples, and not call them to serve the kingdom. It is not only unfaithful, it is absurd.

Yet the Western church, under the influence of revivalism, has consistently done that for the last century and more. Evangelism has been separated from disciple-making. This has led to evangelism programs which stress commitment to Christ without demanding that those who come to him show the fruits that befit repentance. This makes a mockery of discipleship. To understand discipleship in purely personal and privatistic terms, even if we extend it to the realm of interpersonal relations, is to speak of a kind of discipleship Jesus wouldn't have recognized. Discipleship isn't something extraneous to our everyday lives. It deals with how we live in society, how we engage in economic activity, and how we pursue justice and peace.

It is with discipleship that we must be concerned when we evangelize. To be a disciple is to be a learner, one who learns from Jesus. We have much to learn from Jesus. What can we learn from him, the evangelist *par excellence*, about how to evangelize? I propose six learnings for us.

First, Jesus' evangelism was dialogical. As Masumi Toyotome shows us, in the encounter between Jesus and the Samaritan woman at the well, the woman spoke as often as Jesus did, and her words have equal importance. Only once in the seven exchanges did Jesus begin to preach a sermon. He spoke 175 words (in the Greek text); she spoke 122. This is not unusual in Jesus' personal encounters; he listened as much as he talked. "Even the Son of God," Toyotome exclaims, "who surely had more to say than could possibly be expressed in his short ministry on earth, took time to listen attentively to undistinguished persons. For us, who have far less to say than Jesus, the ratio of talking to listening should be far more than half and half."[24]

Second, Jesus' evangelism was situational. The evangelistic stories we read in the New Testament don't show any one pattern. Jesus himself, and not only the apostles, seems to have used a pluralistic approach. He starts from a situation, not a proposition.[25]

Third, Jesus evangelism was servant-evangelism. How do we get into situations in which we will find the persons with whom we are trying to communicate? Scripture tells us that Jesus "emptied himself" (Philippians 2:7). He took "the form of a servant." He "pitched his tent among us" (John 1:14, translation by E. V. Rieu). A modern-day follower of Jesus, the veteran Pentecostal evangelist David DuPlessis, says, "Since I'm after the lost, trying to find them, I have to get lost for sure."[26]

Fourth, Jesus' evangelism was expectant evangelism. There can be a certain latent paternalism even in the most impressive instances of self-emptying evangelism. I may seem to be emptying myself, "sitting where they sit," but I don't really expect I will have anything to learn from those I meet. Jesus was truly amazed by the centurion and the Syrophoenician woman. For DuPlessis, "getting lost" involves expectancy of what he will discover when he gets outside the church. "The Holy Spirit," he believes from his experience of evangelizing over a lifetime, "is more active and gets more consideration and recognition outside of the church than inside."[27]

Fifth, Jesus' evangelism produced conflict. Whenever there is genuine, frontier-crossing evangelism, the responses of those newly reached will "question the validity of that form of the gospel to which they are responding." "Because the good news is *news* it cannot be a repetition of something *déjà vu.*"[28]

It's time now to ask more specifically what that might mean. I've found Segundo extremely helpful here. He distinguishes between Jesus' approach and that of the Pharisees. The Pharisees can't pass judgment on any historical context, even when they're in the midst of it, unless they can deduce an understanding of it wholly from past revelation. They won't take a risk. In order to deal with any new phenomenon, they have to divest it of all its concreteness and specificity.

Jesus, on the other hand, didn't believe certainties could be deduced from revelation. He didn't insist that he needed to operate with certainties. Recall how he responded instantly to the woman taken in adultery (John 8:1-11). Similarly, Jesus' actions on the Sabbath, legal violations according to the Pharisees, show the risk of operating without a previously laid-down certainty. Segundo points us to the incident of the healing of the man with the withered arm in the synagogue on the Sabbath (Mark 3:1-5). The Pharisees were watching to see whether Jesus would heal the man on the Sabbath so they could bring a charge against him. Note that Jesus placed himself within a context where God's already revealed law allowed the Pharisees to make a direct and irrefutable judgment on him, on the basis of theology itself, for their theology taught how the Sabbath was to be regarded.

To the Pharisees' surprise, however, Segundo writes, "Jesus rejects the possibility of forming any concrete judgment on the initial basis of theology or its realm of competence. He asks a purely human question, "Is it permitted to do good or to do evil on the Sabbath?" It's not the kind of abstract question the Pharisees could handle. They had no theological criterion with which to answer it. All they could deal with was whether it was possible to do anything at all on the Sabbath. So they "had nothing to say," Mark tells us. "Jesus' question," Segundo believes, "points up a level which is prior to any and all theological questions, a level where human beings make their most critical and decisive options, i.e., the heart."[29] The conflict between Jesus' approach and the Pharisees' is a complete one.

Segundo goes on to talk about the Pharisees' request (in Mark 8:11-12) for a sign from heaven. I've always found Jesus' answer extremely difficult to understand: "Why does this generation ask for a sign? I tell you this: no sign shall be given it." It's important, Segundo feels, that we understand the context in which the Pharisees were asking for the sign. Jesus had, according to Luke 11:14-16, been driving out a dumb devil. Some people were astonished, but others had an immediate rejoinder—Jesus was doing this by being in league with the devil. A difficult question. How can it be answered with certainty? Perhaps, if Jesus will only give a sign from heaven, then it will confirm that this earthly sign, the healing of the deaf mute, was kosher. But all Jesus does is say, "In the evening you say, 'It will be fine weather, for the sky is red,' and in the morning you say, 'It will be stormy today; the sky is red and lowering.' You know how to interpret the appearance of the sky; can you not interpret the signs of the times?"

Jesus points the people to the necessity of being willing to read the signs of the times with boldness. "He tries to show them that they must leave room and openness in their theology for the relative, provisional, uncertain nature of criteria that human beings actually use to direct their lives in history when they are open to what is going on around them."[30] Jesus seemed to be saying that when human beings "stop at theological certitudes, those certitudes fall apart in their hands."[31] He modeled a more open way of relating to reality. This brought conflict between himself and the religious authorities.

The best example of this kind of reading-the-signs-of-the-times evangelization that I've run across came in the report of a conference held in Zambia in October 1978. It was sponsored by the Africa Region of the World Federation for the Catholic Biblical Apostolate.[32] The conference dealt with evangelization. Among the questions the conferees discussed was how to approach people who have largely been secularized, who show no willing faith. They are receptive neither to the gospel nor to its ministries.

The conferees suggested that the Bible is filled with testimonies of how God's people related to their contemporaries simply in terms of what was going on in their times. Now there's a tremendous ambiguity in all human movements and events. The conferees didnt' want to deny this, any more than Segundo does. We may see a movement for justice and dignity and would like to discern in it the movement of the kingdom, the presence of the Spirit. But, mixed with all the positive aspirations, come negative aspirations as well—the search for power, the desire for revenge, class and ethnic hatred. To read the signs of the times we've got to be critical. We should expect to find both positive signs and negative signs in current history, signs of the Spirit's presence but also signs of its absence, signs of the kingdom, but, alongside those, signs of the demonic.

But can we, they asked, come closer to those movements, closer to the people of our times? Can we come close enough that we can prayerfully discern, in Christian community, what God seems to be doing and interpret that to them? The conferees considered contemporary African reality. They saw movements toward liberation and justice, equality and unity, solidarity and dignity. Such movements, the Scripture tells us, have been signs of God's historical activity in the past. Can we see them as positive signs of the kingdom today? Can we not see the Spirit as present within them?

Alongside these movements, though, they saw movements in the opposite direction. It was easy work to compile a list of "negative signs of the times": apartheid, alcoholism, injustice, exploitation, inequitable distribution of wealth, militarism, tribalism, and corruption. These might seem enough to defeat any kingdom movement. Even with such a negative list, the conferees felt they could begin a process of evangelization. They could work with people to analyze contemporary slaveries. Then they could bring the light of the gospel to bear on them, exposing them for what they are.

Similarly, in the opposite direction, by identifying the "kingdom movements" and "kingdom qualities" in present-day happenings, we can point people to the presence of the Spirit. These are not just human movements, we can say. The Spirit is present in them, among you. We can encourage people to hope. Our goal is that they recognize that their struggle is not merely a human struggle. We yearn for the day when they can exclaim, "Look! God's kingdom is present among us!" I think we can learn much about evangelizing our contemporary Western society by following the lead of the Zambia conference. In chapter 5 I will follow their negative strategy: analyzing contemporary slaveries and bringing the light of the gospel to bear on them.

But one extremely important part of their perspective needs yet to be mentioned. In authentic evangelism, they said, the church must do a lot more than point people to what God is doing outside of it. "God's people," they said, "have a specific and unique function in determining the shape and presence of the kingdom in today's society." And that's not only by our participation in the liberating movements of our times. As a church we are called to be "a living experience of the kingdom, forging friendships, sealing a covenant, growing in fellowship." We must be the sign and instrument of the new fellowship in Christ. Through us God seeks to communicate with an alienated world. As people respond to our outreach, some will seek to attach themselves to our covenant life, coming into a new relationship with God in Christ.

And that, it seems to me, is the *sixth* thing we have to recognize about Jesus' method of evangelism: Jesus sought to knit people into a new society, the new Israel, which would itself be a sign to the times.

When we put together these six aspects of Jesus' discipleship-evangelism, what do we have? Jesus' "doctrine of evangelism"? A "master-plan of evangelism by the Master"? No, nothing so grand. All I have done is discern in Jesus' concrete, historical encounters characteristics which seem to commend themselves to us in our concrete situation. In another generation, in another culture, I would probably compile a somewhat different list.

The list, I thus recognize, is neither complete nor exhaustive. Nor can I pretend to have been "objective" or "presuppositionless" in singling out these features. Nor have I compiled a list which the whole church everywhere at all times should seek to embody. No, for I have a definite sense of who we are and of what our times are like. In these times and in this place I have a sense that much of our evangelism is alienating and that it is largely extraneous to contemporary life. In the six aspects of Jesus' evangelism, which I have lifted up, I discern an approach which might strengthen our evangelism, which might help us reach beyond barriers, and help us communicate with those whom we are not reaching today.

But in order to explain that I must go deeper into an analysis of our society as we enter the eighties.

CHAPTER 5

Religion and the Culture
of Narcissism

The challenge is before us. Can we develop a contextual evangelism for proclaiming the good news in the Western world today? Are we willing to risk the conflict within ourselves and in the church in order to do this? Can we develop a kingdom-oriented evangelism in a world and church in which kingdom-proclamation is unsettling if not unwelcome? Can we do this expectantly, hoping to learn new things from the good news?

If we are strongly based in faith and not in passing ideologies, and if we are willing to take the risks that faith permits us to take, I believe we can. Our evangelism will be a cruciform evangelism, not a triumphal one. We can take the risk to develop it because we believe in the forgiveness of sins. We can take the risk because we believe that the power of God which raised Jesus from the dead is still at work in us today (Ephesians 1:19-20).

I propose that the way to develop such an evangelism is to begin by reading the signs of the times in our current cultural and social setting. In this chapter I will look somewhat deeper at the "neopaganism" I met when I returned to the United States from Ghana in 1970. I want to show that what we have called neopaganism is the religious side of a larger cultural phenomenon, which has been called "the culture of narcissism."

In my local library I found a little volume which helped me take a quick "Cook's tour" of the new spiritual movements which have blossomed through the seventies across the United States. It's called *The New Consciousness*. It was compiled by Armand Biteaux[1] in much the same way that Dave Jackson compiled his guide to Christian communities.[2] For each listing Biteaux gives a brief description of the group's philosophy, a biography of its leaders, and information on how to get in touch with the organization.

The groups are highly diverse, ranging from established groups like the Unitarian-Universalist Association and the Esalen Institute to groups that major in parapsychology and witchcraft. Alongside quite orthodox Eastern religious bodies Biteaux lists groups which specialize in new, Western techniques like biofeedback and groups which are devoted to communicating with visitors from outer space. Obviously I couldn't construct a single ideal type to represent them all. The majority of the groups, however, seem to fall in the category about which Visser't Hooft wrote his essay on the new paganism. It was most interesting, yet disturbing, to see how these groups fit the profile which he drew up.

I made notes of the recurrent features in their philosophies. Many of the groups made such a strong point of having "no dogma, no doctrine, and no creed" that I was quite amused to see how like unto one another they are. The groups are devoted to "self-realization" and "personal fulfillment," to help people discover their "creative potential," to become "spiritually aware." They claim to be able to lead their adherents to "transcendent freedom" and "psychic insight," to states of "divinely human consciousness." One group promised it could show people "how to regenerate your body and experience well-being." Another said it could tune you in to "the voice of truth within yourself."

I detected a keen sense of expectancy in the write-ups. We are coming, one guru wrote, to "the final stage of increased awareness," to the "emergence of the ultimate man." Many of the groups spoke of this as the "emergence of the ultimate man." Many of the groups spoke of this as the "Aquarian Age." We are undergoing, they said, "a revolution in thought." What is going on is a process of "evolution" to a "higher consciousness," an "expansion of human potential."

Some of the groups seemed quite esoteric. They would not admit all comers. Others seemed anxious to evangelize everyone. They would do all in their power to get the good news of higher consciousness out, so that all can come to live in "peace, beauty, joy, perfection, and harmony."

Their methodologies of achieving the new state of being differed greatly. Some seek to instruct us in the proper use of astrology, others in diet, others in types of meditation, others in the use of the I-Ching, the Qabalah, Tarot cards, witchcraft, and "magick." Several of the groups spoke of how they see sex as the symbol and embodiment of life and a source of energy to be used both in magical practice and religious worship. The Kandalini Research Foundation said it was its conviction that "Higher Consciousness depends upon a different brain and nervous system than is possessed by normal human beings." It uses "all legitimate spiritual disciplines to awaken a dormant energy in the body to effect the subtle changes in the nervous system and brain that make Enlightenment possible."

One group, which specialized in communication with "superior visitors from other planets who are assisting in the transition of Earth to a higher frequency level," said it used "telepathy, telethought, tensor beams, and Light Beam." Other groups were more pedestrian, claiming that they aimed simply at helping people achieve "a harmonious eco-psychic relationship with the total Biosphere of Holy Mother Earth" or some such thing. The groups shared a sense that, as one put it, "Man is basically good and has the potentiality for spiritual and aesthetic perfection." The problem is not sin but ignorance. We need to become "intuitive," "fully aware," "autonomous."

Many of the groups claimed an appreciation of the Christian heritage, but said that it needed to be seen from a new perspective, less limited, less world-rejecting. "Every man," one group claimed, "is an individual Christ." We need to "contact the Christ-self within us." Some of the groups were very negative about other religious traditions. The Church of the One in Mendocino, California, for example, which has developed "a Unified System of Magick," says that magic has to be "freed of the gods, devils, angels, spirits, mysteries, and other superstitious mishmash which occultism has accumulated over the years."

The promise of physical healing was held out by many of the organizations. Many of them had a strong sense of the need to be involved in serving the world, in spreading love, and bringing about "understanding and brotherhood among all peoples." They wanted to work for "the betterment of society." The Council of American Witches in St. Paul, Minnesota, feels akin to many progressive Christian groups today. It wants "to define modern witchcraft in terms of the American experience and needs."

This selection of cult promises presents only several of the many such options in the current scene. But it's enough to convey the picture of a diverse, certainly creative, continent-wide movement very different from the churches we know.

Or is it? In our local library the occult section merges into the section on Christianity and Judaism. A few feet away I saw a book entitled *Peace of Mind through Possibility Thinking.*[3] My first thought was that one of the occult books had gotten misplaced. I pulled out the volume. The smiling face of Robert H. Schuller, pastor and founder of the Garden Grove Community Church in California, greeted me. His arms were extended, beckoning me to come. "Let's check this out," I said to myself, and I took the book home.

The book begins:

> Tension seems to be our constant companion in the stress-torn world. The inner calm that is our birthright is continuously assailed by noise, pollution, inflation, illness, personal problems . . . and a myriad of other debilitating experiences. . . . The tension produced in our mind and spirit often results in mental and physical illness and the inability to effectively achieve our life goals.

Schuller goes on to promise, "In this book I will show you the way to eliminate tension from your life and replace it with peace of mind, achieved through possibility thinking."[4] It was uncanny how that promise fit in with the promises I'd just been reading. I read on:

> Our Creator has, like a brilliant cosmic architect, designed an incredible organism called "Human Being." In His basic planning God conceived of engineering within this person a built-in tranquilizing system so relaxed and at peace, that every person would be sensitive and receptive to receive daily spiritual communication from the Creator.

Schuller calls that insight "bio-realism."[5]

Just as the different sects in Biteaux's book gave their

diagnosis of why we don't achieve our full human potential, so did Schuller: "The human being is in an ecologically, psychologically, and spiritually polluted environment"— "thrown into a foreign jungle of cars, buses, concrete, and asphalt," instead of living in "his natural Garden of Eden." It's because we are out of our natural habitat that we are "intellectually and emotionally confused," and that many people have become unbelievers.

Now Schuller knows that he's got something not everyone has. He isn't selfish. He really wants to share it. I thought of different kinds of people I know in Philadelphia, in Northern Ghana, and of people in the slums of Latin America about whom I'd been reading that morning, as I read Schuller's questions to all of us:

> How would you describe your life in emotional terms?
>
> Are you happy-go-lucky? Or uptight and tense?
>
> Do you feel pleasantly relaxed or squeezed by many pressures?
>
> Do you go to work on Monday morning cheerful and optimistic or gloomy and fatigued? (*I thought of the 50% of Philadelphia's black youth who are unemployed.*)
>
> Do you find your enthusiasm turning into despondency?
>
> Are you seldom really joyful—but more often grimly satisfied or gravely anxious? (*I thought of the desaparecidos, the people who have disappeared in Argentine and Chile, if they might be where they could hear these questions.*)
>
> Do you find negative emotions and upsetting and unsettling thoughts dominating your mind most of the time? (*I thought of the farm workers who are being squeezed out of their employment as state universities develop new breeds of vegetables which can be harvested mechanically.*)
>
> Is your life today less than satisfying and do you often feel mysteriously unhappy? (*I could imagine all of the foregoing saying, "No mystery about it."*)
>
> If so, you may be living with enthusiasm-draining, mind-

confusing, life-restricting tensions. *("Damn right!"* they would say.)

And what did Schuller have to say to all of them?

> You may be one of those who are being kept from having a fruitful, stimulating, wonderful, happy life because tension is dominating your inner self.
>
> It is only when a tension-tortured person replaces inner turmoil with a quiet, peaceful, and harmonious center that innate powers are released *(those same "innate powers" I read about in the cult book!).* Then it becomes possible to realize dreams, to think creatively, to reach exciting goals, to live and to live joyously.[6]

Now it's certainly not fair to Schuller to read his book while thinking about such poor people. After all, their problem is not that they are restless and unsatisfied in the midst of affluence, like most of those whom Schuller is addressing. They ought not listen in when he addresses his kind of people.

Or shouldn't they? They might find it interesting. They would find out, for example, that Schuller tells his middle-class flock, "God wants you to prosper."[7] And he isn't interpreting that spiritually—he means in terms of money. He says it in a section on how to deal with tension arising out of scarcity of money. (The first thing to realize, he says, is that "few people have money problems, almost always it's a management problem.")

He tells his people that the way to get ahead through possibility thinking is to stop denigrating themselves.[8] He tells them that "nothing is more important than peace of mind." And he calls it "the pearl of great price."[9]

They would be interested to hear that Schuller advised his flock to commit themselves to "a great cause." It will give them a sense of belonging and a sense of self-identity. He doesn't care what the cause is. Whatever one chooses—religion, politics, the environment, humanitarian causes, they should "participate, get out into the limelight. Assume responsibility. You'll generate self-love, because responsibility fills the need to be needed, and self-love, that wonderful sense of well-being, comes when we know that our life is making a contribution. . . ."[10]

They would find it instructive to learn the theological basis of the architecture of Schuller's church. Schuller's architect wanted to design a building "so close to nature that we will give the Creator a chance to use the built-in tranquilizing system again. We shall block out the ugly power line with solid walls; we shall throw open windows to the big sky! We shall bring the gentle sound of water into the place of peace. Tranquilized, relaxed, we shall be receptive to the natural flow of God's creative thoughts."[11]

They would find it touching that Schuller still has to recommend even to those who have heard his message for a long time a nightly process of "ventilating"—emptying the mind of negative thinking.[12] They would find it sad that, even after an experience of worship, Schuller cautions folks not to go to a place which is too out of harmony with the atmosphere he has set. "The rain that has fallen must be given a chance to soak in the soil." He recommends a restaurant "with cloth napkins, soft voices, and gentle sounds, so the mood of the morning should not be rudely interrupted before the tranquilizing experience has a chance to seep to the deepest levels and farthest corners of the mind."[13]

I don't think those I've imagined listening to Schuller's counsels to his flock would be terribly upset or even surprised. "Those cats have got problems!" they would probably say. "Haven't we been trying to tell you that all along?"

For myself I am embarrassed to hear the good news of

Jesus Christ abused in this way. It would be all right if
Schuller simply said, "I'm not going to preach the gospel,
but a form of middle-class self-help." I could view what he
does with the equanimity with which I regard most of the
cults we looked at earlier. But the man actually thinks he is
telling people how to be born again. "Your life will be so
transformed" (by possibility thinking), he says, you will
literally be 'born again.' "[14] But all he is preaching is the
worst sort of consumeristic religion, pandering to the prejudices, needs, and perceptions of narcissistic individuals.
Instead of selling them cologne, he is selling them religion. I
would say it is a form of syncretism if I could find the Christian elements in it. Perhaps the best term to describe it is
"Christo-paganism," a term missionary anthropologists put
together to describe folk religion in ostensibly Christianized
societies like Latin America.

But I suspect that my reaction is superficial and impercep-
tive, that it doesn't help us at all. After all, people responded
similarly to Norman Vincent Peale, but it did not lessen his
appeal. If we deal with Schuller and the neopaganism of our
times only from a cultural perspective, we won't get very far.

The problem of much contemporary middle-class culture
in the West is not ultimately a cultural problem, but a social-
structural problem. "We sometimes deal with advertisers,"
Dorothee Sölle writes,[15] "as if they were a new god. But
[that's to] give them too much prestige. They are not the
god of a new religion—they are just its priests.... Through
[them] the god addresses us." Who is the god? "The god itself," she writes, "is capitalism." The religion of advertising—and of much contemporary neopaganism and other
forms of consumerism—is the religion of capitalism.

Capitalism is an economic system which—for its own survival
and profit—has to catch our souls into the golden prison of

> buyable things. The purpose of advertising is ... to sell the
> products produced in the capitalist system. . . .
>
> In advanced capitalist societies, advertising's role is refined
> further. It does not merely sell products. It creates a climate in
> which selling, buying, bargaining, and saving become the
> most important human activities. . . . Advertisers know the
> truth of the biblical injunction, "Where your treasure is, there
> will your heart be also." Therefore, advertising tells us where
> our treasures ought to be.[16]

The focus of advertising is not, Sölle explains, on our common human needs. Advertising substitutes private needs for common ones. "The people advertising addresses are just immense egos, manipulated by the language of dreams, wishes, and hopes." That, I feel, is what we have to recognize about the people Schuller addresses, about those whom Biteaux presumes read *The New Consciousness*, and about those who are following one or another alternative in the vast supermarket of neopagan religion.

But what is it about our human psyches that makes us ready victims of such consumerism? A fundamental anxiety, a sense of vulnerability, a need to protect ourselves. This leads us into certain "reflex-attitudes," like, for example, our attempt to put others down in order to secure our own positions. It is our tendency, e.g., as "high brow" people, to condemn "middle brow" and "low brow" people. This is a tradition with a fairly long heritage in the United States. Those who see themselves as possessed of a superior culture condemn the hoi polloi, the "hopelessly middle-class," and the "bourgeois." Though they may like the ice-capades, we go to symphony concerts. Though they spend long hours "glued to the tube," watching without discrimination whatever comes on, we spend our evenings reading poetry or, if we watch at all, watch selectively.

In Christian circles we repeat the same game—we wouldn't dream of taking a Cecil B. DeMille biblical extravaganza seriously. We turn away with disdain from "Jesus junk." Our cars don't sport "Honk if you love Jesus" bumper stickers. More likely our bumper stickers express opposition to nuclear power or support of ecological concerns. In many ways we express our sense of superiority over "ordinary Christians."

I think it could be demonstrated without too much difficulty that much of what we do in our "alternative Christian movement" parallels what the majority Christian community does. All of us are concerned to manage the impressions we give to others. We cannot live without admiring audiences. The world is our mirror. "How are we doing?" we always want to know. We are more concerned, I suspect, with the impressions our performance makes on others than with how well we are actually doing in living out our Christian obedience.

I say this not to criticize but to point to our basic anxiety. We share this anxiety with the vast majority of middle-class people of our time. It is a mark of our culture. The anxiety leads to this behavioral syndrome. But what is the basis of the anxiety?

Christopher Lasch has called it narcissism. In his book, *The Culture of Narcissism*[17] he shows how insights from current psychoanalysis about narcissism can help us understand our cultural malaise.

Remember Narcissus? He was the figure in Greek mythology who happened to see his own reflection in a pond in the woods. He was so entranced by what he saw that he couldn't stop looking. Psychoanalysis has borrowed the figure of Narcissus, as it borrowed Oedipus, to describe a type of personality. Freud's basic insight was that narcissism

is not really self-love, but self-hatred. The infant's initial
world is simply an extension of his or her ego. When it learns
that its parents are not simply at its beck and call, it
experiences a jolt, an insult to its concept of self. It responds
with a boiling rage. Humans normally adjust to this dis-
covery, but some persons' development is arrested at this
stage.

Psychoanalysts found persons coming to them who
displayed a personality disorder for which the term narcissism seemed apt. These persons relate to others in such a
way that it becomes clear they are really relating to
themselves, since the others represent some aspect of their
own selves. Narcissists do not really relate to others at all. In
recent years narcissists have become the psychoanalysts'
dominant type of patient. Once psychoanalysts spent most
of their time dealing with severely repressed, morally rigid
persons. Nowadays they are confronted most often with
chaotic, impulse-ridden characters. Such persons avoid getting closely involved with others. Instead they tend to
cultivate a protective shallowness in their emotional relations. They tend to have acute feelings of oral deprivation.
Many are sexually promiscuous. Often they are hypochon-
driacs.

Woody Allen has played narcissistic personalities so often
that many of you will know the kind of person I am speaking
of. Narcissists wonder whether they are real. They complain
to their analysts of a sense of inner emptiness. They are
dissatisfied with their lives. Often they attach themselves to
strong figures whom they admire, and whose acceptance
they crave, because it makes them feel supported. Yet this
parasitic relationship is not really a relationship—narcissists
fear becoming emotionally dependent. It is easier for them
to handle instantaneous intimacy than long-term depth.

They do not want to make commitments.

When the analysts get to know them, they usually detect a deep, boiling rage seething within them. But they cannot handle this rage. They fear their own appetites and needs and throw up defenses against them. They experience fantasies of omnipotence. They believe they have a right to exploit others and that others should gratify them. Narcissists tend to crave vivid emotional experiences—whatever will convince them they are alive and real. But they are unable to mourn. They are terrified of growing old and of death.

Narcissism is a sickness, a pathology. Don't expect to go out and identify ten narcissists in the next two days. But "pathology," Lasch writes, "represents a heightened version of normality." If narcissists are filling the analysts' couches, then the culture itself is probably tending in the direction of narcissism. While it is not at the pathological stage, Lasch feels it is well advanced.

As he surveys the contemporary scene, Lasch finds in our culture the signs he would expect—in industry, education, sports, the family, the arts, in relations between the sexes, and in movements such as those we have been describing. People are after psychic survival and self-preservation. Though we speak in peaceful language of "cooperation" and "the pursuit of pleasure," Lasch sees a deep power struggle going on under this peaceable mask: "Personal relations has become a cult. It conceals a thoroughgoing disenchantment with personal relations." Everyone is trying to find out how to manipulate others. We do it with one another, as Eric Berne and others have pointed out. Industrialists do it to their workers. Parents are taught to do it to their children."

Lasch thinks it is an illusion that we are learning to be

open and cooperative, that we cherish others' freedom and
autonomy. In reality we are becoming masters of manipulation. The advertising industry is only the most successful at
it. The voice tells us we are the god's special protege—
"We've reserved it for you." "We know you're that rare
person who won't be confused—or compromised—with the
ordinary." "You deserve a break today." "Have it your
way." Advertising knows how to twist us around its—or
rather, capitalism's—finger. But our society as a whole is
learning the tricks.

Lasch does not go into a deep analysis of how this narcissistic culture arose. For this reason people, including
former President Carter, have drawn illegitimate conclusions
from the book. They use it in the way I spoke of a few
minutes ago—to heap blame on people. But that is just
another instance of "blaming the victims."

Lasch has no doubt but that the ordinary people did not
"create" a narcissistic culture. He sees its basis in monopoly
capitalism. In a very real way, he says, we have little control
over our lives. Our lives are shaped for us by the managerial
and professional classes. They constitute the new dominant
class of our society. They administer the system in such a
way that they and the finance capitalists who are behind
them will derive most of the benefits.

Lasch is frustrated by the fact that we resist a class analysis
of modern society. We can see the system of corporate capitalism, but the class that administers it is hidden from us.
For any one who makes the effort to find out who controls it,
the evidence is there. Making no such effort, we fail to see
how our present difficulties arose, why they continue, or
how they might be solved. Instead we have retreated into
private worlds of jogging, bellydancing, and psychic self-
improvement, into cults and sects and other worldly religion.

Instead of trying to change the conditions under which we work, we seek to brighten our lives by buying new goods and purchasing new services.

We are under the impression, which the dominant class seeks to foster, that we are free: "You've come a long way, baby!" But what has actually happened is that the most pervasive form of social control—the subtlest form imaginable—has been imposed on us with our connivance. If we are nevertheless ill at ease, it is just a sign that we need "therapy." We live in a no-fault society. There's no wrong, no punishment for our failure to conform, only "therapy."

We live in a system in which authoritarianism has presumably vanished, Lasch writes. The old lines of authority, patriarchal, familial, ecclesiastical, and generational, have, it is true, been largely delegitimized, invalidated. But a new form of authority exists. It is seen in advertising, and in the educational system, and in the media. With it comes a new form of dependence—on the corporations and the state.

How far we have come from the days when philosophers rhapsodized on the theme of "freedom" and what it would bring! In the end is this what "democracy" means—a situation in which aristocracy has simply been replaced by a less viable, but just as repressive form of control? We tend to think that we are not repressed. Repression is something, we think, which takes place in the Third World and in communist countries. We, however, live in the "free world."

Paolo Freire, whose major work has been in repressive Brazil, points out how people in the industrialized nations are not controlled by violent physical repression. We are kept from the free exercise of our humanity more subtly:

> In the industrialized countries other strategies are required. Violence and physical repression are not the means of op-

pression; on the contrary there is "social well-being," efficiency and order in which the mass media play an important role in masking reality. The education system and the mass media become sophisticated means of social control.

Most frightening of all is the level of alienation in which we become robots without even realizing it, marching to unspoken orders and failing to challenge the reason why. We are dehumanized, unable to express our feelings or even our fears. We are afraid to be human. We become trapped in a vicious circle in which we hide our feelings and then suffer because we are afraid to let them out.

Only radical social change provides the possibility for things to happen in a different way. The more the new society is able to resist the temptations of "consumerism," which characterizes the capitalist way, and manipulation, the more it will be able to build up new human relationships based on a different material reality.[18]

I agree with Freire's diagnosis. I also believe we need to work for radical social change. But I think that unless we have a deeper analysis, a more theological analysis, of the nature of contemporary unfreedom, a new social order will not solve our problems. It is likely that one type of slavery will be replaced by another. To read the signs of the times in the deepest way we have to get beyond cultural analysis, beyond social analysis, and analyze the new paganism and the "culture of narcissism" theologically.

That is what I shall attempt to do in chapter 6.

CHAPTER 6

The Idolatry of Power

To read the signs of the times is, in a certain sense, to do cultural analysis, to analyze society. But it is also more than this. Reading the signs of the times requires theological analysis of what is happening in our times. It means asking the God-question, that is, what does it say about the relationship of modern society to God that it acts and structures its life in such ways? What is God's response to modern life? At what points is God acting, moving to transform human life, delegitimizing certain structures, moving to establish others?

Jacques Ellul reads the signs of the times to indicate that God has abandoned humankind: "God has indeed turned away.... His word as such is no longer being spoken." He finds God absent from our history, our societies, our cultures, our science, and our politics. "God has turned away from us and is leaving us to our fate."[1] He finds in our age signs of an absence of hope and an attitude of scorn or derision, of self-assertion. Because we have lifted ourselves up and scorned and derided others and God, God has abandoned us.

It is almost impossible to convince people in North America that you are serious if you quote Ellul. They are programmed to understand our American world as thoroughly religious. We live in a nation "under God." Ours is a religious people, they say. They associate the "American way of life" with monotheism and think of atheism as something connected with "communists, radicals, and women's libbers."

For a people who have so closely associated the Godhead with their way of life, it seems a joke if you tell them that their way of life is a sign that God has abandoned them.

It is even more ludicrous to suggest that God has not abandoned their society, but that God is to be found in those forces which are working to disestablish their society, the forces working for liberation from militarism, from masculine sexism, from white racism, and from capitalism. To make such an assertion is to say that their god is not God at all, but an idol, that God is a God of liberation working to destroy the empire of their god.

In other words, we are not simply talking of two different conceptions of God, but of two gods—or three or four or more. To be more exact, we are speaking of the true God and idols.

But to think in this way requires shifting gears. The Western world thinks idolatry is no longer a problem. But "can we really say," Segundo asks,

> that polytheism and idolatry have been uprooted from Western culture? Is that true in strictly scientific terms?... We do not mention or allude to different gods by different names any more. Instead we simply use the one word "God" to refer to any and every type of religious experience, even to experiences which are quite contrary to one another....

But Segundo says we have to be willing to describe false, nonexistent gods as false, as projections of human self-assertion:

The innermost tendencies and desires of man tend to crystallize almost of themselves around God. . . . The social and historical tendencies through which he is living also tend to crystallize in his concept or idea of God. In short, man fashions God out of the materials which go to make up his own experienced or imagined socio-historical triumph. . . .[2]

To speak of triumph is to admit that a conflict is going on in history, a struggle of power. Different forces are seeking to possess, to control, to dominate. Those in power, the Latin American Catholic bishops said at Puebla, "absolutize" and "divinize" their power. Power in itself is not evil; it is "a basic part of the order of creation," but it becomes demonic when it is absolutized in modern "national security states." They called on the church to work to "liberate our people from the idol of absolutized power so that they may live together in a society based on justice and freedom."[3]

The bishops hold out hope, in other words, of another kind of society, a society where justice and freedom are present, a society which is truly community. Such a society will be a society where God is present. The present "Christian" national security states are atheistic regimes, they declared.

Their analysis is of the Latin American situation, but it has relevance for us. For a long time we in North America have thought of atheism as a "religious matter." We tend to analyze oppression and injustice in a secular way, on a purely human level. We think they concern human relations alone. The bishops challenged this kind of analysis, and this is where they speak to us as well. If oppression and injustice exist, then it's because of idolatry, the true atheism. Idolatry and atheism have immediate consequences for this-worldly human relationships.

Let me try to apply their analysis. I have tended to look at the "Christian right" of the United States as a "socially conservative or reactionary" group. I have seen their support for militant American chauvinism as a political option. The bishops make me think something more is at stake. I need to criticize the Christian right not just socially and politically but on basic theological grounds. In calling for a "moral majority," these people are not simply trying to give some "silent majority" more political oomph. They are seeking power—power to impose their morals, their concept of authority, their concept of "right living" on the populace as a whole. They are seeking to bind the forces that are calling for change in our society. They want to "go back" to an America of their dreams, where government does not intervene in the socioeconomic realm on behalf of the poor and oppressed, where those with power are not required to be socially responsible, where racism and sexism and the distribution of wealth and income go unchallenged, and where one can be sure that the status quo will remain that.

Their theistic moralism is the ideological underpinning for such a society. Their religion has no place for a liberator God. As Segundo wrote, they assign all of their prior values to God. Around these values their concept of God crystallizes. There is thus no easy way to distinguish between their values and their god. Their god doesn't stand over against their values. He is not superior to them, but their slave. He has been domesticated.

It is a sign of our unfreedom that we cannot tolerate the free Yahweh. Enslaved people of necessity produce an enslaved god. Those for whom current history is an absolute produce a god who does not transcend history, but is its inner driving force, a deistic god rather than the free God of the Bible. This god stands behind the class stratification, the corporate capitalism, the racism and sexism and the homophobia of the Western world. It is the justification for the systemic violence which characterizes Western society. It legitimates the domination of the many by the few, as it goes on today.

One night during the last months of the Carter administration I was watching the Jerry Falwell show. Anita Bryant spoke. She accused those who propose legislation to decriminalize homosexual relationships between consenting adults of being "anti-American, anti-life, and anti-God." What did the three have to do with one another? I wondered. If you define life as the Bible does, God is certainly "pro-life," I recognized. But in what sense could it be said that God is "pro-American?"

As I was still puzzling, Jerry Falwell moved up to the pulpit. "The precious freedoms we've known for so long are slipping through our hands," he began. Whose freedoms was he speaking of? Who was included in the pronoun *we?* I wondered. I knew Falwell was a minister, but he didn't seem to be speaking of "we Christians." His subject wasn't Christian freedom. He went on: "We want our children and grandchildren to know the America we know"—and, before his voice fell, he quickly added: "God bless America!" I then knew who the *we* were.

I, too, I realized, want God to bless America. I, too, cherish America's freedoms. I believe it is God's will that people in society should have the right to express themselves and associate freely. I believe in the Bill of Rights.

Falwell says he does, too. But he is worried that because of our misuse of freedom—"in abortion, pornography, homosexuality, and amorality"—we will lose it. Why? God will take it away. In fact God may have begun to do so. That, Falwell thinks, is why America's power has declined in the world.

It is God's will, he explained, that America be militarily strong. He applauded President Carter's promise to increase the defense budget by 12 percent. Falwell would have been happier had the president increased it by 100 percent. He has no problem knowing where the extra money could come from. It is scandalous, he said, that we are spending one hundred billion dollars more on health and welfare (Falwell's figures) than on defense—"God help us!"

At that point Falwell knew that much of his audience would think he was getting into politics. "I'm not political," he assured us. "I'm dealing with moral issues. The trouble is they've made moral issues political." As a result, no line exists anymore between the moral and the political.

In 1979 Falwell discovered that "95.8 percent of all Americans were on the side of Bible morality." He took that to be a mandate. He started up a campaign to "Clean up America," to "bring this nation back to God." Falwell believes America has a simple choice: "Either revival of America and the fundamentals she was founded upon or the evil sins threatening our country will eventually destroy her."

A couple of days later a piece of Falwell's direct mail promotion arrived at my house. I learned that if I joined Falwell's "I Love America" Club, I would get five things: (1) my own beautiful "Old Glory" flag lapel pin, (2) my personal "Collector's Edition" of "America's Bicentennial Bible" with the Liberty Bell on its cover, (3) a subscription to the "Clean up America *Hotline Report*" (4) "personal" letters from Falwell outlining the plans and progress of the campaign, and (5) a subscription to Falwell's news magazine. (Later I learned I would also get solicitations to support Falwell's Liberty College and his Liberty Missions Society.)

But I am given pause. Falwell, I have an uncomfortable sense, isn't just trying to build up a vast "electronic church" which he can milk economically. He has much greater designs. He is trying to latch onto power. He wants to be a world-historical mover. He has gained immense power, it seems, to influence others. Through extremely skillful use of the media, through intense direct mail advertising, he is building a power base. And he is doing it through the skillful manipulation of Christian symbols. As Segundo wrote, he "fashions God out of the materials which go to make up his own experienced or imagined socio-historical triumph."[4]

It is a false god in whom Falwell believes—a god of military power, unchecked consumerism, capitalistic domination, and authoritarian morality. It is not the God and Father of our Lord Jesus Christ, but an idol.

Now you may have been tempted to respond before the 1980 United States national election by saying I was choosing an aberration, someone on the far right, to support my contention that our current problem was idolatry. But the "Christian right," as the election showed, was anything but an aberration. Candidates who advocated that America had to be "number one, second to none," were swept into office across the country.

But let's not be deluded into thinking that the election marked a major change in the United States' self-understanding. Let's be more critical. Remember that when Jimmy Carter came into office in 1977 he called for a foreign policy of concern for human rights and reduced reliance on military force. By the time he had been in office for a couple of years he had begun to speak instead of the need for a "new militancy." It was he who proposed cutbacks in crucial human programs long before Reagan did, though not at the level Reagan has. It took the Joint Chiefs of Staff by surprise.

They did not even have plans ready for how they would
spend the military funds he wanted to give them. Was no
idolatry involved? Did the "Carter doctrine," that the
Persian Gulf was vital to our security, that we would even go
to war to protect its "independence," not go beyond
geopolitics? Was it not something far more serious? Was it
not a fundamental theological assertion about who is ultimate in the world?

In early 1979, before the troubles in Afghanistan, before
the taking of the hostages in Iran, Carter made a major
speech on foreign policy at Georgia Tech.[5] Those who
thought Carter's later position was totally new would do well
to read it. In that speech we find the ideological basis for
everything he did in the last year of his presidency. "We
now face a world very different from the world in which I
came of age," he began. "The old empires are gone," he
said, "the maps are covered with new, developing nations
with names we had never heard.... But one thing has not
changed.... It is still a world in which democracy and
freedom are constantly challenged." Carter did not define
democracy and freedom. Nor did he say how the passing of
the empires is related to challenging these values.

But then he went on to say, "Disturbances in Iran, the
Western Indian Ocean, and in Southeast Asia are a
challenge to our determination and our leadership." How?
Why? He didn't answer. "They underscore," he said, "the
importance of strength in our national defenses." Defense?
How could something that happened in those remote parts
be related to the defense of our nation?

An answer was forthcoming: "I want to speak to you to-
day," Jimmy Carter said, "about America's role and
America's purpose in this world of change and turbulence."
He defined that purpose by making several claims:

1. The U.S. is the leader in moving the world closer to stable peace and genuine security; he didn't say how.
2. The U.S. has the world's strongest economy.
3. The U.S. has the world's strongest military; we "share burdens of defense mutually with friends abroad whose security and prosperity are as vital to us as to themselves." (So that's how "our defense" was related to events taking place elsewhere.)
4. With our allies we prevent global war.
5. We "help to sustain a world trading and monetary system that has brought greater prosperity to more of the world's people than ever before in history." He didn't defend this claim. He didn't speak of those peoples who were less well off in 1980 than they were when that world trading and monetary system developed. He didn't speak of those, like China, who were better off than they were when they were the victims of that world system.
6. We are working to resolve conflicts among other nations, and
7. We have helped maintain the conditions in which more than one hundred nations have newly come into being and in which human hope has taken a revolutionary leap forward. He didn't speak of how we resisted the growth of independence in many of those countries. He didn't say that we sided regularly with oligarchies and juntas which kept human hope down, and with dictators who opposed "revolutionary leaps" with torture and repression.

Carter concluded: "We provide the bedrock of global security and economic advance" in the world.

That was Carter's angelology. His demonology followed. "We see the darker side of change when countries in turbulence provide opportunities for exploitation by outsiders" (remember, United Brands and the U.S. Marines are not outsiders, but friends) "who seek not to advance human aims but rather to extend their own power and position at the expense of others" (unlike us).

He then went on to explain how these principles guided us in our involvements in countries around the world—Iran, Southeast Asia, the Middle East. In all these places, he said, "We will protect the vital interests of the United States." To what extent? "There must be no doubt," he said, "that the people of the United States are fully prepared to meet its commitments, and to back up these commitments with military strength."

The crucial point, the basic presupposition lacking exegesis, is that our spoken ideals—working for peace, democracy, and national independence and prosperity— were tied up with our commitment to "the vital interests of the United States." This meant we would support the ideals only insofar as they were consistent with our vital interests. The vital interests dominated. They colored how we would pursue the ideals, if at all. That was obvious to anyone who watched our foreign policy. Carter, just like Reagan, combined high-sounding rhetoric with self-centered power-maintenance. But could such a combination be legitimately made? Could we be a force for genuine peace and still pursue our own interests?

Peace, full peace, which requires justice and leads to the fulfillment of human potential, requires change. The United States, for many presidencies, has not stood for change but for stability. "The determination and strength of purpose of the American people are crucial for stability in a turbulent world," Carter had concluded in his speech. This nation stands for stability, and that means the status quo, or as close to it as we can get. We stand for the maintenance of a system which is in our interests, unjust though it is. The "peace" we want is the absence of any conflict which threatens the present world system, which threatens the alliance between internal elites in Third World countries and our multinationals, and which threatens the present economic order among nations. If ever a nation had a chance to support by peaceful means a new and more just international economic order, the U.S. has had this chance through the processes for a New International Economic Order at the United Nations.[6] But for years we have been dragging our heels, along with our "friends" in Western Europe and Japan.

It is time to say it once more. The problem is ultimately not one of foreign relations. The problem is one of idolatry. We cannot serve the peace of God and Mammon. Either we will hate the one and love the other, or we will love the one and hate the other.

As Jim Stentzel puts it:

> We think we have a right to live in the style to which we've grown accustomed. Increasingly in today's world this means that . . . other peoples have fewer rights. Despite all the rhetoric about human rights, our lifestyles dictate a foreign policy ruled not by respect for the rights of others but by our own economic self-interest.[7]

Jim and others like him reaffirm what the confessing church had to say in Germany a generation ago: "We repudiate the false teaching that the church, in human self-esteem, can put the word and work of the Lord in the service of some wishes, purposes, and plans or other, chosen according to desire."[8] God's gracious will can't be delimited by our "national self-interests." To do so is to make our national self-interests come first. It is to make of them an idol.

We're beginning now to come to the point where we can see that the challenge is an evangelistic challenge. The problem is not one of a socioeconomic system which just needs reordering. It is a theological problem. The primary level on which the problems need to be addressed is the level of belief systems.

What we have in our international military posture is the same phenomenon we have in our narcissistic culture as a whole: the power-struggle is concealed under a thin rhetoric of "cooperation" and the desire for others' freedom. The reality is that we not only don't sense ourselves bound to any significant others, but we are also positively outraged by the fact that we have to depend on them in any way. We are terrified of being vulnerable, terrified of weakness, and terrified of death. We believe we have a right to exploit others, that others should gratify us, but we resist them. We have fantasies of omnipotence, but deep within we feel inauthentic, empty. We are chaotic and impulse-ridden.

All the "solutions" for which we reach, whether in the personal realm or in the field of international affairs, are dead-ends. Americans' inner emptiness is not going to be satisfied by hedonism and pagan or Christo-pagan religions of "self-actualization." America's emptiness as a nation is not going to be satisfied by another generation of exploiting poor nations nor by inflicting armed terror on our enemies.

Yet we cannot be reasoned into giving up our ways. We don't use the systems; they use us. Social institutions are greater than the sum of their constituent parts. Once established, organizations and structures gain a life of their own. They are what the Bible calls "principalities and powers." They cannot be reasoned out of existence. Their nature is to oppress, to alienate, and to imprison. If those who are bound by them are to be liberated, the devils must be cast out.

That's why the synoptic Gospels always associate the preaching of the good news with the exorcism of demons. Preaching and exorcism are not two fundamentally separate tasks, as we in our secularized world-view tend to think. Those of us who are inclined to do evanglism and social justice divide our tasks into two separate activities: preaching the gospel and working for social justice. A kingdom-oriented evangelism, one which truly reads the signs of the times, will see them as one task, not two. Structures of injustice and militarism cannot be taught out of existence, but preaching is not just teaching. Preaching involves a word of power. It is a demeaning view of evangelism which says people cannot be effectively liberated from such structures by the preaching of the word. But how such preaching will do this, what kind of a word it will be, and how will it be communicated are the questions.

We're at a frontier, I sense, when we begin to think in this way—the frontier of a new holism, in which the proclamation of the word and the liberation of humanity from the sway of the principalities and powers are no longer set over against each other. They are seen as integrally related. I've encountered little in my reading to indicate that people have begun to grasp this possibility. One seminal article seems to have blazed the trail. It's by Jürgen Moltmann and Douglas Meeks, and it's entitled "The Liberation of Oppressors."[9] Let me share its analysis briefly; it describes three expressions of America's neopaganism.

Viewing oppression as sin and conversion as liberation from oppressive systems, Moltmann and Meeks use three examples of systems that oppress. They oppress not only those we generally think of as oppressed, but their oppressors as well. The systems are racism, masculine sexism, and capitalism.

Racism is a structure in which the characteristics of one's own race are identified with human being itself. Persons of other races are seen as subhuman. Racists use their own race's characteristics to justify themselves, to enhance their self-value, and to explain their right to dominate others.

The inner aspect of racism is that it is a mechanism for self-justification. Its outer, ideological aspect is that it is a mechanism for subjugating and dominating others. Because of an underlying anxiety we justify ourselves in such a way that we dominate others, destroy community, and destroy ourselves. Racists' "despising, insulting, and subjugating of others," the authors write, "is basically self-hatred."

Masculine sexism is similar. It is men's pride in their own sex, their shaping of culture to favor men's special characteristics and devalue presumed "feminine" attributes. It is their putting women down as "the weaker sex" and excluding them from full participation in society. Like racism, masculine sexism is a form of self-justification. Complete human being to the masculine sexist means masculine being. For men to identify themselves in this way is to identify themselves negatively and aggressively: men are "not women" more than they are men ("What are you doing, Billy, crying? Don't be a woman!").

The inner aspect of masculine sexism is that it is a mechanism of self-justification. The outer is that it is an ideological mechanism for subjugating and using the other sex. Men's superhuman pride expresses a deep and inhuman anxiety. Those who identify being human with being male destroy themselves, destroy women, and destroy human community between men and women. Masculine sexism is basically self-hatred.

Capitalism oppresses us in a similar way. Not only does it oppress those whom it uses; it oppresses those who run the system and benefit from it. Who ever falls under the compulsion of capitalism will be alienated from his or her true self. They will always have to justify themselves by means of success, work, profit, and progress. Capitalism tells them human beings are what they accomplish: "You are nothing! You must work to become something!"

Capitalism depends on accumulation of wealth, but wealth that is so saved up cheats people of loving, vital lives. Capitalism further isolates us from one another. The possessing classes can enrich themselves only at the cost of the laboring classes. Affluent nations maintain their standard of living only at the cost of poor nations. Capitalism, like racism and sexism, therefore destroys human community. But it even destroys community within the ruling classes. Competition guarantees that individuals will finally be left alone in a world they are taught to regard as hostile.

"Racism and sexism," Moltmann and Meeks write, "are most dangerous when they are combined with capitalism." Capitalism's drive for "permanent, unlimited increase of power and mastery" combines with similar drives in racism and sexism. All three systems are rooted in deep anxiety, in self-hatred. This issues in aggression, in self-assertion.

You can already see why Moltmann and Meeks call this a theological problem. What we are dealing with is nothing less than original sin. "The manifold acts of sin," they write, "are rooted in the one sin of distorted existence." Ultimately, they are sure, we cannot address any sins unless we address sin. They are talking about original sin.

The authors point out four dimensions of the classical Christian doctrine: (1) Human beings do not merely *have* sins; they *are* sinners. (2) Sin is not a moral error but a *compulsion,* a servitude of the will. (3) This distorted mode of being and compulsion are *universal.* (4) The doctrine of evil as sin is a *doctrine of hope.* That's because it doesn't see sin as our fixed human destiny but as our history. It can be overcome by God.

They go on to explain how sin originates. Original sin, they say, is really nothing more, but nothing less, than a miscarried love of God. If we withdraw from God the love that we as human beings have been created to give God, if we direct it toward that which is not God, several consequences follow: (1) These finite things cannot satisfy our love. (2) Out of disappointment, we destroy these finite things. (3) We become greedy to possess and gain a mania to dominate. Love which is disappointed in its expectations turns into a rage for destruction.

At this point, according to Paul (Romans 1:24-28), God's wrath appears, not as punishment but as abandonment. God "gives us over" to our perverted senses.

We imagine that we are free, because we are following our desires. But our perverted desires do not satisfy us. "The essence of historical human being is a passion for love." As Ernesto Cardenal writes,

> In the eyes of all people glistens an unquenchable longing. For the sake of this love, all crimes are committed and all wars waged; for its sake, people love and hate.... The unquenchable love of dictators for power and wealth and possessions is in truth the love of God.[10]

"Sin," the authors comment, "is nothing other than the perversion of the love of God." It won't work, therefore, for us to appeal to people to recognize what they are doing and expect them to change.

> If the oppressor acts under compulsion, if the sinner has lost his or her freedom, then moral indictments and appeals do not help.... The oppressor's relationship to the ground of his or her existence, to the abandoned God, must be changed. But it can be changed only from this ground itself, only by God. It *has* been changed by God.... According to the New Testa-

ment the *humanity of God* is revealed in the messianic mission, in the sacrifice, in the suffering and dying of Jesus. God humiliates himself, lets himself be wounded, draws the deadly aggression upon himself and becomes the victim in order to free the oppressor from the compulsion to humiliate others.

According to the New Testament the *divinity of humanity* is revealed in the resurrection of the crucified Jesus.... God's rule frees the human being from sin and suffering and forms that community free of anxiety in which there are no longer masters or slaves. (Galatians 3:28).[11]

How can oppressors be liberated, be humanized? Moltmann and Meeks give a radical answer: through faith.

The oppressor discovers himself or herself in the crucified Jesus.... The oppressor discovers the God whom he or she has loved with despair.... In this pain of God on the cross the sinner's aggression comes to an end. In this suffering of God the divine love for a miscarried creation is revealed. In this sacrifice of God the gracious justice of God is created in the unjust person.[12]

We are justified freely by God's grace (Romans 3:21). That is what we learn when we hear the evangel. That alone can truly liberate us. But if that does not liberate us, then we must question whether justification by God's grace has really been preached. The freed person can no longer conform to the scheme of this world. He or she is "dead" to the demands and rewards of the world of oppressors. "In the cross of Christ," Moltmann and Meeks write, "the freed person dies to racism, masculinism, and capitalism. The new, free human being is born. He or she is identified as a human being and abandons the fixed narrow identifications of his or her race, class, etc." Those who are truly freed are freed to live in community with other human beings, with themselves, with nature, and with God. Instead of seeing freedom as mastery—a freedom which led them to prison— they now see freedom as "unhindered solidarity and open communion."

I thought of the end of the story of the healing of Legion as I read these words (see chapter 1). The end of the exorcism is that Legion is restored to community. Instead of having to live among the tombs he goes back to his friends (Mark 5:19).

Many of the signs of our times tell us of the breakup of community in our modern Western world and of our alienation from one another. What Moltmann and Meeks have described with such profundity is a kind of cultural-social exorcism in which persons are freed from the demons—of racism, sexism, and capitalism—which have driven them apart. They are freed from the passion to dominate, from compulsive aggression, from slavery to self-destruction. They are freed *for* community. At its very core the gospel is a message of social reconciliation. It is the gospel of the kingdom, of a new social order, the order of community which God is establishing.

It's not by a second step that we go from personal salvation to social reconciliation. But it is a second step to go from reading the signs of the times to theological reflection. "Theology comes after," Gustavo Gutierrez has written.[13] Theology is the second step which follows after a critical analysis of our context. The context we have analyzed presents us with a definite challenge: how do we respond to the idolatry, to "neopaganism," the practical atheism of our times? How will we cast our evangelistic message and approach?

In the final chapter we will address this question.

CHAPTER 7

A Contextual Evangelism for the Western World Today

Ve live today," the Sicilian nonviolent activist Danilo Dolci said in a recent address in Philadelphia, "in an equipoise between despair and presumption." On the one hand people are tempted to give up; on the other, they continue to mouth presumptuous claims no one has a right to advance anymore: the situation is so grave that it precludes easy answers. As we read the signs of the times in the West today, we are in danger of being long on diagnosis and short on prescription. The situation is so overwhelming that we are likely to become paralyzed.

But we dare not. The kind of analysis we have been dealing with is hopeful because, unlike much analysis, it goes deep enough to get to the root of it all—human sin. Once we are at that point, as Christians we have resources. As those who believe in the forgiveness of sins, we will not end up saying, "There's nothing that can be done. It's hopeless. The world will always be a jungle."

No, something *has been* done. God has dealt with human sin. We can announce the good news.

Moltmann and Meeks did not intend, in that one short article, to draw a picture of what the proclamation of that good news will look like today. That task is ours. The kind of theological analysis they and others provide leads me to four concrete implications for evangelism: (1) Evangelism will arise out of a community which lives out the message of God's grace. (2) Evangelism involves both proclamation and celebration. (3) Evangelism will be specific, not general. (4) Evangelism is oriented toward the kingdom of God.

1. *Evangelism will arise out of a community which lives out the message of God's grace.* The community which proclaims the word in the Western world today must confront the basic fact that that world is horribly divided. It is a world of real conflicts—class divisions, divisions of race and sex and age. It is also a world in which the individual actors are terribly fragmented. A community which wants to proclaim the good news of Jesus Christ in such a world will therefore need to be a community which itself transcends the divisions which plague that world. It will be a community which brings together people of different ages, sexes, classes, races, parties, and nationalities. It will be a community of people who have found the key to a wholeness the world does not have, a community of whole people who are not fragmented into souls and bodies, workaday lives and Sunday lives, individual existences and community life.

This does not mean that the community needs to have solved all the problems which plague the world in order to evangelize. We would be a long time waiting for such a community! But it will need to be a community which is open to the freedom God is bringing into human life. That means it will not be conformed to the orders and divisions of this alienated world. It will steadily seek to be transformed by God's renewing power.

It will not have domesticated the Bible. So many today have made the Bible into a rationalization for the world's

present divisions. They use it to proclaim the legitimacy of
what is illegitimate. The community will rather be one
which has come to terms with the otherness of the new
world the Bible speaks of. It will see its charter in the future
rather than in the status quo. It will understand that God is
now at work to break open the fixities of human alienation,
to bring about a new order of freedom.

As a member of Jubilee Fellowship I am for the first time
in my life coming to be able to say what Africans said to me
in the sixties about the meaning of being human: "I am because I participate." Jubilee Fellowship is not a voluntary
association to which I belong. It is my family. Its members
are my sisters and brothers. Having come to live in the same
neighborhood, we share our lives together. We no longer
just "go to church." Sunday morning is no more "church" to
me than Wednesday afternoon or Friday night.

I do not make vocational decisions any longer on my own.
Nor do my wife and I raise our children on our own. We do
these things in community. Our brothers and sisters share
with us in such responsibilities. We also share with them.
Much that used to belong to what the world calls the private
sphere is for all of us part of community life. Whether it's
counseling one another or doing home repairs, we no longer
have to function as isolated individuals.

This gives us strength. Much of the West's highly touted
freedom and autonomy is really, as Paul Tillich showed a
generation ago, heteronomy—rule by others. We are ruled
by consumerism, by fashions and trends. Modern persons
don't really belong to themselves. They justify themselves
by conforming to others' expectations of what they should
do, have, and wear.

But even an alternative Christian community, we recognize, can become a new sort of alienating authority. We in

Jubilee Fellowship therefore feel it's crucial that we continually test our perceptions by a regular evaluation of our judgments in the light of Scripture and in dialogue with other Christian communities. We seek to discern what God is saying to us in the Bible and through our brothers and sisters elsewhere.

One of Jubilee Fellowship's most healing aspects for me has been its unashamed feminism. It has regularly been women who have challenged the tendency of many of us men to justify ourselves by our achievements, to derive our identity from our vocations. We no longer equate vocation and identity. What we usually meant by vocation in the past was our paid work, our official role. Our roles as husbands, fathers, citizens, neighbors, and even church members were secondary. They did not form part of our sense of vocation.

At the age of forty-three I am finally at the point of seeing that my vocation is to be a human being, a member of a family, a community, a neighborhood. If my job identity is to have any vocational authenticity, it must, I now believe, arise out of a grounding in that vocation. This has led me to a whole new way of being a speaker, a workshop leader, and a writer: these activities arise out of my concrete life-involvement. Now when I go off to a distant city to carry out a speaking engagement that activity is of a piece with my life at home. I am no longer the "distant expert" sharing things with my audience out of erudition, deep study, and fascinating experiences. I am a fellow human being sharing with other pilgrims on the path of life.

One of the areas in which Jubilee Fellowship has not yet fully experienced church, however, is that our fellowship does not transcend race and class divisions or include older people. We wrestle a lot with this. It was because we wanted to live in an integrated neighborhood that we moved to Ger-

mantown from our original homes. But few of us have yet
found friends among the more than 60 percent of our
neighbors who are black. Although most of our neighbors
are blue collar workers, we've not got a plumber or factory
worker among us. We're very middle class, very intellectual,
and very white.

To some of us this means Jubilee cannot constitute our
whole definition of church. Our sense of church must include a larger Christian community as we relate to Christian
groups beyond us who include people of other races, classes,
and ages. Though our fellowship continues to try to attract
such people, we begin to be aware that we cannot wait till
we have had success in doing so before we find ways of relating to the whole church. Jubilee, like ourselves, will only be
insofar as it participates in Christ's larger body.

2. *Evangelism involves proclamation and celebration.*
Many people have spoken of the need, in an alienated world
such as the one we live in, of Christian "presence." In place
of a consciously kerygmatic, proclamatory style of Christian
engagement in the world, they call for Christians to be more
concerned just "to be there," to be "the church for others."
Some who speak in this way hold out the hope that the
world, seeing Christ's love incarnate in the church, will
come to inquire about Christians' faith. Then opportunity
may arise for conscious verbal witnessing. Even if this does
not happen a kind of "implicit evangelism" is going on, they
say, as the church seeks to live out its life as "salt for the
world."

I appreciate the importance of what such people have
been saying; the church has had much too facile a word for
too long a time, and much too halfhearted a commitment.
Our lifestyle as Christians makes an implicit witness, it is
true, but it seems to me it is a half-truth. Evangelism must at

some point become consciously and verbally kergymatic. The world we described in the last chapter does not know God's love. It cannot intuit it. Its every inclination is in the opposite direction. While the church should show penitence for its past manipulation of persons, it cannot go all the way to the opposite extreme and make no effort to express its hope in words. As David Killian writes:

> Confessing faith in God means that inarticulateness is not ac-
> ceptable for a long period of time. We may go through
> periods of confusion and transition in the church and in our
> own thinking, but there is something fundamentally wrong
> with saying, "I will wait until I get my act together or until
> the church gets its house in order before I confess faith in
> God." While I might hope for a greater articulateness later, I
> still must attempt a confession now, stammering as it might
> be.[1]

Because our verbal expression is halting at best, it's a good thing that our proclamation isn't limited to the preached Word. Our tongues may be tied when we try to speak the Word, but our proclamation is not limited to such stammering. Something else is at the center of the community's life. It is also a form of evangelism. That is celebration—in word and song, in dance and embrace, in eating and drinking and washing with water. The liturgy "speaks" and proclaims, empowers and frees.

It seems to me that one sign of whether a community's evangelism is rooted in celebration or not is the number of "musts" the community uses. A community which is rooted in celebration of the liberating love of God will show it in its language. Its language is one of permissions—of "cans" and "mays"—not of "musts." It lays no "heavy trip" on people, but invites them to experience God's freeing grace.

Another sign of such a community is the presence of a good sense of humor. Because the community believes that the kingdom is ultimately of God's bringing, not ours, it is freed from the anxiety of ultimate responsibility. Whatever the power of the enemy, we know that power pales before God's victorious grace. Such a faith can be effectively freeing.

Radical Christians are often seen as humorless people, intensely earnest, hardworking, but not grace-filled. Although we have rejected the Protestant ethic as far as it applies to upward mobility, job-performance, and personal accumulation, we seem to have transferred it to our efforts toward social justice. I see something happening, however, in the radical communities I'm familiar with. That's a new emphasis on celebration and on the inward journey of self-discovery in relation to God. Out of this is coming a new trust in God, a recognition that the time-schedule is God's, not ours, an ability to laugh, to relax, to trust.

Something *happens* nowadays in our worship experiences. We no longer gather on a Sunday to hear a moral imperative but to worship God, to give praise, to offer our lives, and to receive them back transformed. We go to embrace one another, to forgive each other's sins, to intercede on one another's behalf, to break the Word for one another.

I have a sense that when all this has really soaked in (and it is a comparatively recent development for some of us), our efforts at verbal evangelism will be charged with new power. Up until now we've gotten through mostly to people very much like ourselves. We communicate effectively with those who are looking for a more radical form of discipleship than they have found in the established churches. We have not been adept, however, at speaking the Word to those who have not sought us out.

It does no good to say to us, "Why don't you just preach the gospel?" What we have seen of evangelism has often been an evangelism without the gospel, a form of cheap grace and culture religion. It has no attraction for us. We sense that biblical evangelism must be radically different from much contemporary "soul winning." Until now we've not found a style we can adopt, one we feel is authentic. Perhaps, and this is my hope, our new experiences of celebration will lead us to one.

But I sense another development will do this as well. Many of us in Jubilee Fellowship are discerning that God is calling us to exercise our Christian obedience in a more dispersed style than we had expected—as part of secular coalitions and groups. We're looking beyond our alternative Christian organizations; we have a sense that God is calling us to do more than set up new biblical institutions. While much of our work will continue to be addressed to doing that, we realize we don't have the answer to all of Germantown's and Philadelphia's problems.

We see at the same time that the Spirit has touched many people in our city and neighborhood to work for the same kingdom values and kingdom goals as we do. Many of them are not Christians. To work with them we have to go outside the boundaries of our Christian organizations and institutions. We go out to work alongside folks who are sacrificially working for justice, for the dignity of the poor, and who are trying to build up community. May it perhaps be that, in working with such people, we'll find a way to communicate the gospel verbally? Beginning by reading the signs of the times alongside others we may find the way to the kind of authentic evangelism we're searching for.

In a lecture delivered in Chicago in 1979[2] Douglas John Hall spoke of what it would mean for the church to take up a "prophetic model" of engagement in today's world. "From our Constantinian past," he said, "we have inherited a quite predictable set of rules which permit us to go only so far" in our relation to outside secular groups:

1. The church can support movements and causes which are clearly within the realm of conventional Christian morality. (This means that many causes are eliminated *a priori* from Christian participation, e.g., the gay movement, and aspects of the women's movement.)

2. The church can support these other groups so long as its identification with them does not compromise the church (i.e., so long as fraternization with such groups does not get the church into trouble with its primary support group, which usually means the dominant middle-class culture).

3. The church will take part in activities involving other groups provided it can maintain a clear organizational autonomy and (still more desirable) a clear-cut authority. It would be better, in fact, according to this mentality, for the church itself to be the initiator of any such mutual activities, so as not to become the victim of manipulation by other groups.

To take up a prophetic model of the church, Hall goes on, would mean to set aside quite consciously these Constantinian ground rules, these inherent reservations about the others:

If God is truly at work in the world "to make and to keep life human"; if God moves mysteriously amongst all kinds of people, using many strange combinations of human energy, emotion, and motivation to accomplish his purposes for humankind, then surely we do not have to be so very careful about our associations as we have been and are. Jesus wasn't. The church that listens to the voice of the Good Shepherd to-

day will inevitably find itself in strange places, with strange
people, doing strange things.... To be the friend of man is
sometimes to wander far away from God—or at least from his
familiar haunts, the holy places beloved by the religious....
The prophetic community will find itself, very often, in the
company of the modern equivalents to publicans and sinners.

I thought about Hall's words last week as I took communion in a very strange place, in an apartment building
which had been abandoned by many of its tenants. I was in
the apartment of one of the staff members of the Tenants'
Action Group, a single parent with two children. She was being evicted because of her efforts to organize the tenants to
demand heat, hot water, and proper building maintenance.

The apartment was jam-packed. We were a very motley
crew—Christians, Jews, Muslims, agnostics, and atheists,
black and white, activists, unemployed people, professionals,
a state legislator, poor and middle class. We had all been at a
meeting the night before and learned that this woman was
to be evicted. As many as could were asked by leaflet to
come to be at her apartment at 8:30 the next morning to
stand between the removal company and the sheriff on the
one hand and the soft-spoken mother on the other.

About a quarter of the previous night's audience appeared. As it turned out, we were able to stop the eviction
without having to intervene physically. Many of those who
came were prepared, however, to do nonviolent resistance if
necessary, to put their bodies on the line for a woman they
did not personally know.

As we sat there drinking coffee and eating donuts to
celebrate the victory, I sensed myself part of that larger flock
Christ spoke of, saying he would still draw them to himself
(Jn. 10:16). There was a sense of trust in the room, a sense of
confidence, a feeling of ease and good humor. I've only

begun to relate to such groups, to get beyond the Christian ghettos in which I lived much of my life. My first attempts to get out were mixed with fear. But I've sensed a freedom when I did so. These people accepted me for who I was, as a Christian. I did not need to hide my faith-commitment. I have a sense that the authentic evangelism I've been hoping for does not lie far ahead.

3. *Evangelism is specific, not general.* It hardly needs saying after all this that evangelism, being directed toward concrete, actual, whole persons, must be specific. In engaging people in dialogue, seeking to read the signs of the times with them, we must be clearly aware of the situation in which they find themselves. We must seek to address ourselves to them.

It is not our goal to master or manipulate people. We don't therefore need to get them onto our turf in order to speak with them. We meet them on their own grounds, for we know that the Spirit of God is at large in the world. We look for signs of the Spirit's presence, specific signs of his activity, as well as for specific signs of his absence as we dialogue about God's good news.

Reading the signs of the times is no simple matter. Different people will read those signs very differently. This will lead to conflict not only with those whose interests we challenge by our reading but also with those in the church who read the signs very differently.

If we stick to generalities, we don't run this risk (in my experience, I don't run into conflict in the church when I speak generally of God's actions. It is only when I become specific that I do.) But a church which wishes to engage in biblical evangelism cannot limit its proclamation to the general. It will not remain, as its "friends" counsel it, above the battle. It will not be able to avoid taking sides. It will find no way of being pastoral rather than prophetic.

We can't find a better example of specific, contextual evangelism than that of the prophet Jeremiah. God had called him, Jeremiah knew, not only to "build up," but also to "tear down," not only to "plant," but also to "root out" (1:4-10). The times in which God called Jeremiah to prophesy were not easy times. Jeremiah was unable to find anyone in Jerusalem who did right (5:1). The streets, he saw, were filled with "evil people lying in wait to attack God's people," wicked people eager to fill their houses with the loot of others (5:26ff.). To plunder the defenseless was the preferred means of becoming wealthy (then as now!).

Jeremiah found that the injustice reached even to the prophets and the priests (6:13f.). It reached beyond them to the king himself, whose concern was not for justice but for conspicuous consumption (22:13-17). Jeremiah read the signs of the times with pain. Throughout his long career it pained him to have to preach judgment, to have to foretell God's punishment (e.g., 4:19-31, 8:18-21). It's an understatement to say he derived no pleasure from having to judge his people. "My sorrow," he said, "cannot be healed. I am sick at heart." Nevertheless he could not bring himself to stop, nor could he change his message to a more cheerful one. Jeremiah, unlike the false prophets, could not say, " 'Peace, peace,' when there is no peace" (6:14). His preaching was not a form of positive thinking.

For many years Jeremiah hoped his words would bring the people to repent and turn to God, so judgment would not fall on them (see, for example, 7:1-7). But while the people kept refusing to heed Jeremiah's call, the time passed during which they could change and still avoid the downfall of their nation. Jeremiah's word therefore changed. He began to counsel Judah to surrender to the Babylonians. It was God's will, he said, that Judah give in, that it not resist defeat (21:8-11; 38:17f.). The reversal of Judah's fortunes was a sign that God had determined to punish the nation.

Jeremiah was attacked and frequently imprisoned. Many simply rejected his word (e.g., 26:8-11). At several points (as in 27:1-11) it was only by symbolic action that he could get his message across. The people would not listen to him anymore (similar experiences have moved many protesters against the arms race in our times to resort to the pouring of blood and ashes). Only shock techniques provided a way of getting the message across. Jeremiah had become a laughing-stock no one took seriously (20:7-9).

Some of Jeremiah's words seemed positively treasonous. For example, he advised those who had been exiled to Babylon in the first deportation to give up thought of returning home in their lifetime. They should instead "seek the good of the city where you are in exile" (29:1-14).

But in the midst of it all, Jeremiah did something that appeared contradictory. From prison he arranged to buy a piece of land in Anathoth (32:6-15). He invested his money in a doomed country! Why? Because his vision transcended Judah's downfall. The Lord had revealed to him that, after Judah's exile, "houses, fields and vineyards will again be bought in this land" (v. 15). He knew that God will "make a new covenant with the house of Israel and . . . Judah" (31:31-34).

Nowadays we tend to dehistoricize Jeremiah's preaching. We look for the "eternal truth." Specific contexts don't interest us. This quick sketch of Jeremiah's career makes it clear, however, that contexts were crucial for his message. A message as specific as his could only be couched in concrete situations. Jeremiah preached no general philosophy of life. His word contained no "eternal truths" but those that took specific forms in historical situations.

We must be just as specific as Jeremiah in our evangelistic proclamation. We will not give the same message everywhere we go. What we say at one time and place will be different from what we say at other times and places. We may have one message for one group of people and another message for a different group. Does United Parcel Service deliver the same package to everyone? God's wisdom, Ephesians tells us, is "manifold"; it has many different forms (3:10).

"Should we look for the essential core of the gospel message?" someone asked Walter Hollenweger at a seminar I attended. "Oh, yes!" he replied. "That is our duty. But we will never find it. God's Word is always moving on before us."

4. *Evangelism is oriented toward the kingdom of God.* As we read the signs of the times, we discern what God is doing in history: bringing the kingdom into our midst, transforming human history into the new creation. God is doing this in the whole of creation. The church is that segment of the creation which acknowledges and affirms this. It does not seek in its evangelism to call people away from the world, into an alienating kind of transcendence, but helps people respond to the transcendent as it impinges upon history.

Those who evangelize in this way know that the pattern of the kingdom is given in the cross and resurrection of Jesus. Only through suffering does the kingdom come to triumph. We seek, therefore, to hear what God is saying especially through the suffering ones in today's world. We try to get "the view from below," knowing from the Bible that God has made a preferential option in favor of the poor. It is in the cross that God's preferential option for the poor becomes the clearest. God's Son becomes one of the poor and oppressed. As the Lausanne Covenant puts it, "The church that proclaims the cross must itself be marked by the cross."[3] An evangelistic lifestyle will be one which involves suffering, that voluntarily takes suffering upon itself.

But God raised Jesus from death. Paul tells us that Christ became in his resurrection the first fruits of a new creation (1 Corinthians 15:20-23). It's God's intention that all should share in Christ's resurrection, that the world shall no longer be bound to the power of death. God is working right now to liberate creation from its thralldom to death.

So when the church's proclamation of God's Word involves denunciation, when the church must pronounce negative judgment, it does so in the context of a larger annunciation. Its "no" is contained within its "yes." It knows that Jesus is God's "yes" to all of his promises (2 Corinthians 1:19f.). He is not "yes" and "no."

Once again this pattern was prefigured in Jeremiah's proclamation. The "no" he had to speak, even against his will, he spoke in the context of a larger "yes," one he had heard from God. Despite their apostasy, he said, Israel and Judah are still God's people. So also those to whom we preach are God's people. By virtue of their election in Christ before all ages (Ephesians 1:9, 11) the people we confront in evangelism are God's people. This is true despite their idolatry and alienation. If we preach judgment, that word is both deadly serious and eschatologically limited.

In a meditation on Jeremiah Lesslie Newbigin draws parallels between Christ's ministry and Jeremiah's and between Jeremiah's and our own. He writes:

> As I think about our society and the calling of the church within it, I wonder whether we do not have to go through a

period like that of Jeremiah when we can offer no solutions but can only call upon our fellow-countrymen to recognize, and accept for ourselves, the judgment of God upon our idolatrous society, putting our whole trust in his power to redeem us in the end out of the bondage that confronts us.

Our stance, though, must be like Jeremiah's and Christ's:

> We make our witness out of a dual stance of dissent from our nation's values—and nonconformity with those values—and solidarity with our society—a recognition that we exist as a church for the sake of our nonmembers.

Newbigin calls on the church to align its common life "alongside all who are the needy, the marginal, the excluded, the unwanted." We will not bear on our bodies "the accolade of worldly success but the marks of the cross." The cross of Jesus, he goes on, "was his supreme act both of dissent and of solidarity. In ... dying ... he exposed our life in the piercing light of God's judgment." He offered us a new hope beyond that judgment.[4]

In pointing to the kingdom, we enter into solidarity with the people of our times, people who are anxious and fearful and yet who seek meaning and authenticity. Many of them strive for a better world. We know of this world through hope. Scripture tells us that not we alone but the whole of creation "is waiting with eager longing" for it and it will in fact come (Romans 8:20-22).

The new world is already coming. By evangelism we "hasten the day of its coming" (2 Peter 3:12). Waiting for the "new heavens and the new earth where justice will be at home" (v. 13), we tell people what we know of that kingdom and call them to align themselves with it.

In its ministry in Amsterdam, to which I referred in chapter 1, Oudezijds 100 has, Pastor Rolf Boiten writes, constantly been tempted to veer in two opposite directions–toward activism on the one hand and accommodation on the other. But the way of the kingdom is neither of these:

> Thank God we do not have to choose between these two possibilities—between, on the one hand, the comfortable egotism of a silent majority and, on the other, the loud (mostly half-) involvement of the crying minority, with whom the Word of the Lord just as seldom is heard.

> There is a third possibility. Moses and his people went this way. When they got to the Red Sea, they went neither to the right nor to the left. They went on the impossible way, straight ahead. Straight into the water of death. And they found—new life.

> It is not the violent change of our dysfunctional structures which will bring us the product of the new man. The New Man already has been revealed. He has said to us, "Whoever sees me sees the Father."

> Whoever lets this world really sink into his heart will follow the third way, the way of the silent minority, described in the Bible as "the quiet of the land." Such a person is a genuine non-conformist; he goes out from the group, "out of the camp. . . ."

Boiten goes on:

> The third way is not the way of quietism ("Christ has already done all—let's go to the church fair!"). But it is also not the way to a kingdom we ourselves must build. It is rather the way on which we simply attempt to give a model of the form of salvation. The model isn't the building itself. But the model gives us an idea of what the building, in outline, will finally look like.

Boiten closes with a moving illustration of what it means to be moving toward the kingdom:

> Somewhere in a remote corner of our Fatherland during the War there was a bicycle mechanic of whom it was said that he was a very strange man. When he met someone he did not know, he always said, "My name is Halbertsma; I am on the way to the kingdom of God. While I am on the way, I repair bicycles." Probably Halbertsma had found the third way: the way of the silent minority. So also we in Oudezijds 100 still remain in that way, "repairing bicycles." For how long yet? Thy kingdom come![5]

Notes

Chapter 1

1. Elizabeth Schüssler Fiorenza, "For the Sake of Our Salvation," in Daniel Durken (ed.), *Sin, Salvation, and the Spirit* (Collegeville, Minn.: Liturgical Press, 1979), p. 30.

2. Christopher Lasch, *The Culture of Narcissism* (New York: Norton, 1978).

3. Lausanne Committee for World Evangelisation, *The Willowbank Report—Gospel and Culture* (Wheaton, Ill.: LCWE, 1978), (Occasional Papers No. 2), pp. 11-12.

4. Ans van der Bent, *God So Loves the World* (Maryknoll, N.Y.: Orbis Press, 1979), p. 114.

5. Public Citizen's Congress Watch, *The Case for a Corporate Democracy Act of 1980* (Washington, D.C., 1980), pp. 29-31.

6. From the original manuscript of an article which subsequently appeared edited as "Poortalk" in *The Other Side*, Vol. 16, No. 3 (March 1980), pp. 10-16.

7. *Ibid.*

8. Pierre Emmanuel, "Réapprendre a Vivre," *Le Figaro*, December 2, 1973 (author's translation).

9. *Philadelphia Inquirer*, February 25, 1980, p. A-3.

10. Ronald Goetz, "Strangely Manifest" in *Christian Century*, December 26, 1979, p. 1283.

11. *Ibid.*

12. William R. Callahan, "Noisy Contemplation," in *The Wind Is Rising* (Mt. Rainier, Md.: Quixote Center, 1968), p. 35.

13. John H. Yoder, "The Contemporary Evangelical Revival and the Peace Churches," in Robert L. Ramseyer (ed.), *Mission and the Peace*

Witness (Scottdale, Pa.: Herald Press, 1979), p. 82.

14. "A Bolivian Manifesto on Evangelism in Latin America Today," in *A Monthly Letter About Evangelism*, World Council of Churches (Geneva) February 1975.

15. Ecumenical Coalition of the Mahoning Valley, *A Response to the Mahoning Valley Steel Crisis* (Youngstown, Ohio: ECMV, November 29, 1977), pp. 3-5.

16. *Ibid.*

17. Catholic Committee of Appalachia, *This Land Is Home to Me* (Prestonburg, Ky., C.C.A., 1975). The quotation is from p. 11.

18. From a privately distributed translation of selected passages from Rolf G. H. Boiten, *Gastfreie Kirche* (Munich: Christian Kaiser Verlag, 1972).

Chapter 2

1. J. C. Hoekendijk, *The Church Inside Out* (Philadelphia: Westminster, 1966).

2. The presentations at the Carter Symposium can be found in Tetsunao Yamamori and Charles R. Taber (eds.), *Christopaganism or Indigenous Christianity?* (So. Pasadena, Calif.: William Carey Library, 1975).

3. A summary of this report, "Evangelism in Mainline Denominations," was published in *Christian Century*, Vol. XCVI, No. 16 (May 2, 1979), pp. 490-496. The whole report is available from Division of Church and Society, National Council of Churches, New York.

4. *The Unchurched American*, Princeton Religion Research Center, 1978.

5. John Stott, "World Evangelization: Signs of Convergence and Divergence in Christian Understanding," *Third Way*, December 1, 1977, pp. 3-9.

6. Wilbert Shenk (ed.), *The Challenge of Church Growth* (Scottdale, Pa., and Kitchener, Ont.: Herald Press, 1973).

7. "Evangelism: Good News or Bad News?" Akron, Pa.: Mennonite Central Committee, 1970.

8. English version in John Eagleson and Philip J. Scharper (eds.), *Puebla and Beyond* (Maryknoll: Orbis, 1979), pp. 123-263.

9. *Ibid.*, pp. 190f.

10. *Ibid.*, p. 191.

11. *Ibid.*, pp. 189f.

12. Jacques Ellul, "How I Discovered Hope" in *The Other Side*, Vol. 16, No. 3 (March, 1980), pp. 28-31.

13. Eagleson and Scharper, *op. cit.*, p. 139.

14. *Ibid.*, p. 222.

15. *Ibid.*, p. 265.

16. *Ibid.*, p. 264.

17. Dean Kelley, *Why Conservative Churches are Growing* (New York: Harper & Row, 1972).

Chapter 3

1. Mircea Eliade, *Cosmos and History: The Myth of the Eternal Return* (New York: Harper & Row, 1959), p. 95.

2. *Ibid.*, pp. 88-89.

3. Source unknown.

4. Karl Löwith, *Meaning in History* (Chicago: University of Chicago Press, 1949), p. 18.

5. Eliade, *op. cit.*, p. 156.

6. Löwith, *op. cit.*, p. 84.

7. Eliade, *op. cit.*, p156.

8. Henry Sumner Maine, *Ancient Law* (Boston: Beacon, 1963), pp. 21-23.

9. Max Weber, *The Protestant Ethic and the Spirit of Capitalism* (New York: Scribner's, 1958), p. 13.

10. Arend Van Leeuwen, *Christianity in World History* (New York: Scribner's 1964), p. 435.

11. My understanding of Chokosi culture and society is presented in my book, *Go . . . and Make Disciples* (London: S.P.C.K., 1974).

12. John V. Taylor, *The Primal Vision: Christian Presence Amid African Religion* (London: S.C.M., 1963).

13. Placide Tempels, *Bantu Philosophy* (Paris: Presence Africaine, 1959).

14. E. E. Evans-Pritchard, *Nuer Religion* (Oxford: Oxford University Press, 1956).

15. W. A. Visser't Hooft, "Evangelism in the Neo-Pagan Situation," *International Review of Mission*, Vol. LXIII, No. 249 (January 1974), pp. 81-86.

16. *Ibid.*

Chapter 4

1. Walter Wink, *The Bible in Human Transformation* (Philadelphia: Fortress Press, 1973), p. 3.

2. John H. Yoder, "The Message of the Bible on Its Own Terms" (Elkhart, Ind.: unpublished paper, 1969), p. 11.

3. John Eagleson and Philip J. Scharper (eds.), *Puebla and Beyond* (Maryknoll, N.Y.: Paulist, 1979), p. 297.

4. Wink, *op. cit.*, p. 8.

5. Juan Luis Segundo, *The Liberation of Theology* (Maryknoll, N.Y.: 1976), pp. 8f.

6. *Ibid.*, p. 108 and Brevard Childs, *The Book of Exodus* (Philadelphia: Fortress Press, 1974), p. xvi.

7. Yoder, *op. cit.*, p. 6.

8. Brevard Childs, *Biblical Theology in Crisis* (Philadelphia: Westminster Press, 1970), p. 107.

9. *Ibid.*, pp. 131ff.

10. "Jesus himself seemed to focus his message on liberation at the level of interpersonal relationships," Segundo writes, "forgetting almost completely, if not actually ruling out, liberation *vis-a-vis* political oppression of the Romans." For Jesus "the decisive and critical political plane—precisely in political terms—wasn't the opposition between Judea and the Roman Empire but between the Jewish theocracy and Jesus." Jesus was eliminated by the Sanhedrin because he was their political adversary (Segundo, *op. cit.*, pp. 110f.).

11. Wink, *op. cit.*, pp. 32-34.

12. Walter Hollenweger, "Evangelism: Good News or Bone of Contention?" in *Evangelism Today* (Belfast, N. Ireland: Christian Journals, Ltd., 1976), pp. 76-97.

13. Eagleson and Scharper, *op. cit.*, p. 67.

14. *Ibid.*, p. 82.

15. *Ibid.*, pp. 81-83.

16. *Ibid.*, p. 332.

17. Hollenweger, *op. cit.*, p. 69.

18. *Ibid.*, p. 93.

19. *Ibid.*, p. 93.

20. Childs, *Biblical Theology in Crisis*, p. 105.

21. Segundo, *op. cit.*, pp. 106-107.

22. *Ibid.*, p. 108.

23. Herbert Gans, *Deciding What's News* (New York: Pantheon, 1979), pp. 29f.

24. Masumi Toyotome, "Love Is Listening" in J. Ogden (ed.), *Going Public with One's Faith* (Valley Forge, Pa.: Judson Press, 1975), p. 25. Walter Hollenweger distinguishes helpfully between evangelists and propagandists. The latter "do not consider that they could learn anything about Christ from the heathen, the agnostic, the indifferent, or—horrible *dictue*—the communist" (Hollenweger, *op. cit.*, p. 69).

25. Hollenweger, *op. cit.*, p. 82.

26. Quoted in an earlier, unpublished version of Walter Hollenweger's essay, "Evangelism: Good News or Bone of Contention?"

27. From the same unpublished essay.

28. Hollenweger, *op. cit.*, p. 93.

29. Segundo, *op. cit.*, pp. 77f.

30. *Ibid.*, pp. 79f.

31. *Ibid.*, p. 80.

32. World Federation for the Catholic Biblical Apostolate, "Report of the First Pan-African Evangelization Seminar," in *Word Event*, No. 34, Sept. 2, 1979, Stuttgart, W. Germany. I have written an article based on an earlier report in *Word Event*, No. 33, in *The Other Side*, Vol. 16, No. 1. (January 1980), pp. 41-46.

Chapter 5

1. Armand Biteaux, *The New Consciousness* (Whittier, Calif.: Oliver Press, 1975).

2. Dave Jackson, *Coming Together: All Those Communities and What They're Up To* (Minneapolis, Minn.: Bethany Fellowship, 1978).

3. Robert Schuller, *Peace of Mind Through Possibility Thinking* (Garden City, N.Y.: Doubleday, 1977).

4. *Ibid.*, p. 7.

5. *Ibid.*, p. 9.

6. *Ibid.*, p. 15.

7. *Ibid.*, p. 102.

8. *Ibid.*, p. 29.

9. *Ibid.*, p. 28.

10. *Ibid.*, p. 39.

11. *Ibid.*, p. 10.

12. *Ibid.*, p. 47.

13. *Ibid.*, p. 168.

14. *Ibid.*, p. 28.

15. Dorothee Sölle, "Consumerism: Opiate of the Masses," in *The Other Side* 82 (July 1978), pp. 53-55.

16. *Ibid.*

17. Christopher Lasch, *The Culture of Narcissism* (New York: Norton, 1978).

18. From unpublished World Council of Churches paper (n.d.).

Chapter 6

1. Jacques Ellul, *Hope in Time of Abandonment* (New York: Seabury, 1973), pp. 71-74.

2. Juan Luis Segundo, *The Liberation of Theology* (Maryknoll, N.Y.: Orbis, 1976), pp. 45-47.

3. John Eagleson and Philip J. Scharper, *Puebla and Beyond*

(Maryknoll, N.Y.: Orbis, 1979), pp. 193-194.

4. Segundo, *op. cit.*, p. 46.

5. In the *New York Times*, February 21, 1979.

6. For an analysis of the NIEO from a Christian perspective, see Philip Land, "Stewardship and the NIEO" in *The Earth Is the Lord's*, ed. by Mary Evelyn Jegen and Bruno V. Manno (New York: Paulist Press, 1978), pp. 100-111.

7. Jim Stentzel, "That Others May Simply Live," in *Sojourners* (February 1979), pp. 3-4.

8. In John Leith (ed.), *Creeds of the Churches* (Chicago: Aldine, 1963), p. 522.

9. Jürgen Moltmann and Douglas Meeks, "The Liberation of Oppressors," in *Christianity and Crisis*, Vol. 38, No. 20 (December 25, 1978), pp. 310-317.

10. *Ibid.*, p. 314.

11. *Ibid.*, p. 315.

12. *Ibid.*, p. 315.

13. In Segundo, *op. cit.*, p. 76.

Chapter 7

1. David Killian, quoted in *Occasional Papers*, Institute for Ecumenical and Cultural Research, Collegeville, Minn., Summer, 1979.

2. "The Church of the Cross," Community Renewal Society and St. Paul's Church, Chicago, 1979.

3. Lausanne Covenant in *Let the Earth Hear His Voice*, J. D. Douglas (ed.) (Minneapolis, 1975), p. 5.

4. Lesslie Newbigin, "The Mission of the Church in England Today," in *Free Church Chronicle* (London), Summer, 1979.

5. G. H. Boiten, *Gastfreie Kirche* (Munich: Christian Kaiser Verlag, 1972).

Appendices

FRANKFURT DECLARATION
on the Fundamental Crisis in Christian Mission
(March 1970)

> "Woe to me if I do not preach the
> gospel!" *(1 Corinthians 9:16, RSV)*

The church of Jesus Christ has the sacred privilege and irrevocable obligation to participate in the mission of the triune God, a mission which must extend into all the world. Through the church's outreach, his name shall be glorified among all people, mankind shall be saved from his future wrath and led to a new life, and the lordship of his son Jesus Christ shall be established in the expectation of his second coming.

This is the way that Christianity has always understood the Great Commission of Christ, though, we must confess, not always with the same degree of fidelity and clarity. The recognition of the task and the total missionary obligation of the church led to the endeavor to integrate missions into the German Protestant churches and the World Council of Churches, whose Commission and Division of World Mission and Evangelism was established in 1961. It is the goal of the Division, by the terms of its constitution, to insure "the proclamation to the whole world of the gospel of Jesus Christ, to the end that all men may believe in him and be saved." It is our conviction that this definition reflects the basic apostolic concern of the New Testament and restores the understanding of mission held by the fathers of the Protestant missionary movement.

Today, however, organized Christian world missions is shaken by a fundamental crisis. Outer opposition and the weakening spiritual power of our churches and missionary societies are not solely to blame. More dangerous is the displacement of their primary tasks by means of an insidious falsification of their motives and goals.

Deeply concerned because of this inner decay, we feel called upon to make the following declaration.

We address ourselves to all Christians who know themselves through the belief in salvation through Jesus Christ to be responsible for the continuation of His saving work among non-Christian people. We address ourselves further to the leaders of churches and congregations, to whom the worldwide perspective of their spiritual commission has been revealed. We address ourselves finally to all missionary societies and their coordinating agencies, which are especially called, according to their spiritual tradition, to oversee the true goals of missionary activity.

We urgently and sincerely request you to test the following theses on the basis of their biblical foundations, and to determine the accuracy of this description of the current situation with respect to the errors and modes of operation which are increasingly evident in churches, missions, and the ecumenical movement. In the event of your concurrence, we request that you declare this by your signature and join with us in your own sphere of influence, both repentant and resolved to insist upon these guiding principles.

Seven Indispensable Basic Elements of Mission

1. "Full authority in heaven and on earth has been committed to me. Go forth therefore and make all nations my disciples; baptize men everywhere in the name of the Father and the Son and the Holy Spirit, and teach them to observe all that I have commanded you. And be assured, I am with you always, to the end of time"

(*Matthew 28:18-20*).

We recognize and declare:

Christian mission discovers its foundation, goals, tasks, and the content of its proclamation solely in the commission of the resurrected Lord Jesus Christ and his saving acts as they are reported by the witness of the apostles and early Christianity in the New Testament. Mission is grounded in the nature of the gospel.

We, therefore, oppose the current tendency to determine the nature and task of mission by sociopolitical analyses of our time and from the demands of the non-Christian world. We deny that what the gospel has to say to people today at the deepest level is not evident before its encounter with them. Rather, according to the apostolic witness, the gospel is normative and given once for all. The situation of encounter contributes only new aspects in the application of the gospel. The surrender of the Bible as our primary frame of reference leads to the shapelessness of mission and a confusion of the task of mission with a general idea of responsibility for the world.

> 2. "Thus will I prove myself great and holy and make myself known to many nations; they shall know that I am the Lord"
>
> *(Ezekiel 38:23).*

> "Therefore, Lord, I will praise thee among the nations and sing psalms to thy name"
>
> *(Psalm 18:49 and Romans 15:9).*

We recognize and declare:

The first and supreme goal of mission is the *glorification* of the name of the one *God* throughout the entire world and the proclamation of the lordship of Jesus Christ, his Son.

We, therefore, oppose the assertion that mission today is no longer so concerned with the disclosure of God as with the manifestation of a new man and the extension of a new humanity into all social realms. *Humanization* is *not* the primary goal of mission. It is rather a product of our new birth through God's saving activity in Christ within us, or an indirect result of the Christian proclamation in its power to perform a leavening activity in the course of world history.

A one-sided outreach of missionary interest toward man and his society leads to atheism.

> 3. "There is no salvation in anyone else at all, for there is no other

name under heaven granted to men, by which we may receive
salvation"
                                    (Acts 4:12).

We recognize and declare:

Jesus Christ our Saviour, true God and true man, as the Bible
proclaims him in his personal mystery and his saving work, is the
basis, content, and authority of our mission. It is the goal of this
mission to make known to all people in all walks of life the gift of
his salvation.

We, therefore, challenge all non-Christians, who belong to God
on the basis of creation to believe in him and to be baptized in his
name, for in him alone is eternal salvation promised to them.

We, therefore, oppose the false teaching (which is circulated in
the ecumenical movement since the Third General Assembly of
the World Council of Churches in New Delhi) that Christ is
anonymously so evident in world religions, historical changes, and
revolutions that man can encounter him and find salvation in him
without the direct news of the gospel.

We likewise reject the unbiblical limitation of the person and
work of Jesus to his humanity and ethical example. In such an idea
the uniqueness of Christ and the gospel is abandoned in favor of a
humanitarian principle which others might also find in other religions and ideologies.

4. "God loved the world so much that he gave his only Son, that
   everyone who has faith in him may not die but have eternal
   life"   *(John 3:16).*

   "In Christ's name, we implore you, be reconciled to God!"
                                    (2 Corinthians 5:20).

We recognize and declare:

Mission is the witness and presentation of eternal salvation
performed in the name of Jesus Christ by his church and fully au-
thorized messengers by means of preaching, the sacraments, and
service. This salvation is due to the sacrificial crucifixion of Jesus
Christ, which occurred once for all and for all mankind.

The appropriation of this salvation to individuals takes place
first, however, through proclamation which calls for decision and

through baptism which places the believer in the service of love. Just as belief leads through repentance and baptism to eternal life, so unbelief leads through its rejection of the offer of salvation to damnation.

We, therefore, oppose the universalistic idea that in the crucifixion and resurrection of Jesus Christ all men of all times are already born again and already have peace with him, irrespective of their knowledge of the historical saving activity of God or belief in it. Through such a misconception the evangelizing commission loses both its full, authoritative power and its urgency. Unconverted men are thereby lulled into a fateful sense of security about their eternal destiny.

> 5. "But you are a chosen race, a royal priesthood, a dedicated nation, and a people claimed by God for his own, to proclaim the triumphs of him who has called you out of darkness into his marvellous light"
>
> *(1 Peter 2:9).*
>
> "Adapt yourselves no longer to the pattern of this present world"
>
> *(Romans 12:2).*

We recognize and declare:

The primary visible task of mission is to call out the *messianic, saved community* from among all people.

Missionary proclamation should lead everywhere to the establishment of the church of Jesus Christ, which exhibits a new, defined reality as salt and light in its social environment.

Through the gospel and the sacraments, the Holy Spirit gives the members of the congregation a new life and an eternal, spiritual fellowship with each other and with God, who is real and present with them. It is the task of the congregation through its witness to move the lost—especially those who live outside its community—to a saving membership in the body of Christ. Only by being this new kind of fellowship does the church present the gospel convincingly.

We, therefore, oppose the view that the church, as the fellowship of Jesus, is simply a part of the world. The contrast between the church and the world is not merely a distinction in function and in knowledge of salvation; rather, it is an essential difference in nature. We deny that the church has no advantage over the world except the knowledge of the alleged future salvation of all men.

We further oppose the one-sided emphasis on salvation which stresses only this world, according to which the church and the world together share in a future, purely social, reconciliation of all mankind. That would lead to the self-dissolution of the church.

> 6. "Remember then your former condition . . . you were at that time separate from Christ, strangers to the community of Israel, outside God's covenants and the promise that goes with them. Your world was a world without hope and without God."
>
> *(Ephesians 2:11, 12).*

We recognize and declare:

The offer of salvation in Christ is directed without exception to all men who are not yet bound to him in conscious faith. The adherents to the non-Christian religions and world-views can receive this salvation only through participation in faith. They must let themselves be freed from their former ties and false hopes in order to be admitted by belief and baptism into the body of Christ. Israel, too, will find salvation in turning to Jesus Christ.

We, therefore, reject the false teaching that the non-Christian religions and world-views are also ways of salvation similar to belief in Christ.

We refute the idea that "Christian presence" among the adherents to the world religions and a give-and-take dialogue with them are substitutes for a proclamation of the gospel which aims at conversion. Such dialogues simply establish good points of contact for missionary communication.

We, also, refute the claim that the borrowing of Christian ideas, hopes, and social procedures—even if they are separated from their exclusive relationship to the person of Jesus—can make the world religions and ideologies substitutes for the church of Jesus Christ. In reality they give them a syncretistic and therefore anti-Christian direction.

> 7. "And this gospel of the Kingdom will be proclaimed throughout

the earth as a testimony to all nations; and then the end will
come"

(Matthew 24:14).

We recognize and declare:

The Christian world mission is the decisive, continuous saving
activity of God among men between the time of the resurrection
and second coming of Jesus Christ. Through the proclamation of
the gospel, new nations and people will progressively be called to
decision for or against Christ.

When all people have heard the witness about him and have
given their answer to it, the conflict between the church of Jesus
and the world, led by the antichrist, will reach its climax. Then
Christ himself will return and break into time, disarming the demonic power of Satan and establishing his own visible, boundless
messianic kingdom.

We refute the unfounded idea that the eschatological expectation of the New Testament has been falsified by Christ's delay in
returning and is, therefore, to be given up.

We refute at the same time the enthusiastic and utopian
ideology that either under the influence of the gospel or by the
anonymous working of Christ in history, all of mankind is already
moving toward a position of general peace and justice and will finally—before the return of Christ—be united under him in a great
world fellowship.

We refute the identification of messianic salvation with
progress, development, and social change. The fatal consequence
of this is that efforts to aid development and revolutionary involvement in the places of tension in society are seen as the contemporary forms of Christian mission. But such an identification would
be a self-deliverance to the utopian movements of our time in the
direction of their ultimate destination.

We do, however, affirm the determined advocacy of justice and
peace by all churches, and we affirm that "assistance in development" is a timely realization of the divine demand for mercy and
justice as well of the command of Jesus: "Love thy neighbor."

We see therein an important accompaniment and verification of
mission. We also affirm the humanizing results of conversion as
signs of the coming messianic peace.

We stress, however, that unlike the eternally valid reconciliation with God through faith in the gospel, all of our social achievements and partial successes in politics are bound by the eschatological "Not yet" of the coming kingdom and the not yet annihilated power of sin, death, and the devil, who still is the "prince of this world."

This establishes the priorities of our missionary service and causes us to extend ourselves in the expectation of him, who promises, "Behold, I make all things new" *(Revelation 21:5, RSV)*.

Unless otherwise indicated, biblical quotations are taken from *The New English Bible*.

This declaration was unanimously accepted by the "Theological Convention," a regular meeting of theologians who want to be faithful to Scripture and confession, at their session on March 4, 1970, in Frankfurt, West Germany.

Among the first signers are the following:

Professor P. Beyerhaus, ThD, Tübingen
Professor W. Bold, ThD, Saarbrucken
Professor H. Engelland, ThD, Kiel
Professor H. Frey, ThM, Bethel
Professor J. Heubach, ThD, Lauenburg
Mr. A. Kimme, ThD, Leipzig
Professor W. Künneth, ThD, PhD, DD, Erlangen
Professor O. Michel, ThD, Tübingen
Professor W. Mundle, ThD, Marburg
Professor H. Rohrbach, PhD, Mainz
Professor G. Stählin, ThD, Mainz
Professor G. Vicedom, ThD, DD, Neuendettelsau
Professor U. Wickert, ThD, Tübingen
Professor J. W. Winterhager, ThD, Berlin

Reprinted by permission of Peter Beyerhaus, Universität Tübingen.

THE CHICAGO DECLARATION
of Evangelical Social Concern

As evangelical Christians committed to the Lord Jesus Christ and the full authority of the Word of God, we affirm that God lays total claim upon the lives of his people. We cannot, therefore, separate our lives in Christ from the situation in which God has placed us in the United States and the world.

We confess that we have not acknowledged the complete claims of God on our lives.

We acknowledge that God requires love. But we have not demonstrated the love of God to those suffering social abuses.

We acknowledge that God requires justice. But we have not proclaimed or demonstrated his justice to an unjust American society. Although the Lord calls us to defend the social and economic rights of the poor and the oppressed, we have mostly remained silent. We deplore the historic involvement of the church in America with racism and the conspicuous responsibility of the evangelical community for perpetuating the personal attitudes and institutional structures that have divided the body of Christ along color lines. Further, we have failed to condemn the exploitation of racism at home and abroad by our economic system.

We affirm that God abounds in mercy and that he forgives all who repent and turn from their sins. So we call our fellow evangelical Christians to demonstrate repentance in a Christian discipleship that confronts the social and political injustice of our nation.

We must attack the materialism of our culture and the maldistribution of the nation's wealth and services. We recognize that as a nation we play a crucial role in the imbalance and injustice of international trade and development. Before God and a billion hungry neighbors, we must rethink our values regarding our present standard of living and promote more just acquisition and distribution of the world's resources.

We acknowledge our Christian responsibilities of citizenship. Therefore, we must challenge the misplaced trust of the nation in economic and military might—a proud trust that promotes a national pathology of war and violence which victimizes our neighbors at home and abroad. We must resist the temptation to make the nation and its institutions objects of near-religious loyalty.

We acknowledge that we have encouraged man to prideful domination and women to irresponsible passivity. So we call both men and women to mutual submission and active discipleship.

We proclaim no new gospel, but the gospel of our Lord Jesus Christ who, through the power of the Holy Spirit, frees people from sin so that they might praise God through works of righteousness.

By this declaration, we endorse no political ideology or party, but call our nation's leaders and people to that righteousness which exalts a nation.

We make this declaration in the biblical hope that Christ is coming to consummate the kingdom and we accept his claim on our total discipleship till he comes.

> (Adopted on November 25, 1973,
> by 53 leaders of evangelical perspective,
> Chicago, Illinois)

From *The Chicago Declaration,* Ronald J. Sider, editor, copyright 1974, Creation House, Carol Stream, Ill. 60187. Used with permission.

THE LAUSANNE COVENANT

(July 1974)

Introduction

We, members of the church of Jesus Christ, from more than 150 nations, participants in the International congress on World Evangelization at Lausanne, praise God for his great salvation and rejoice in the fellowship he has given us with himself and with each other. We are deeply stirred by what God is doing in our day, moved to penitence by our failures, and challenged by the unfinished task of evangelization. We believe the gospel is God's good news for the whole world, and we are determined by his grace to obey Christ's commission to proclaim it to all mankind and to make disciples of every nation. We desire, therefore, to affirm our faith and our resolve, and to make public our covenant.

1. *The Purpose of God*

We affirm our belief in the one eternal God, Creator and Lord of the world, Father, Son, and Holy Spirit, who governs all things according to the purpose of his will. He has been calling out from the world a people for himself and sending his people back into the world to be his servants and his witnesses, for the extension of his kingdom, the building up of Christ's body, and the glory of his name. We confess with shame that we have often denied our calling and failed in our mission by becoming conformed to the world or by withdrawing from it. Yet we rejoice that even when borne by earthen vessels the gospel is still a precious treasure. To the task of making that treasure known in the power of the Holy Spirit we desire to dedicate ourselves anew. (*Is. 40:28; Mt. 28:19; Eph. 1:11; Acts 15:14; Jn. 17:6, 18; Eph. 4:12; 1 Cor. 5:10; Rom. 12:2; 2 Cor. 4:7*)

2. The Authority and Power of the Bible

We affirm the divine inspiration, truthfulness, and authority of both Old and New Testament Scriptures in their entirety as the only written Word of God, without error in all that it affirms, and the only infallible rule of faith and practice. We also affirm the power of God's Word to accomplish his purpose of salvation. The message of the Bible is addressed to all mankind. For God's revelation in Christ and in Scripture is unchangeable. Through it the Holy Spirit still speaks today. He illumines the minds of God's people in every culture to perceive its truth freshly through their own eyes and thus discloses to the whole church ever more of the many-coloured wisdom of God. (*2 Tim. 3:16; 2 Pet. 1:21; Jn. 10:35; Is. 55:11; 1 Cor. 1:21; Rom. 1:16; Mt. 5:17, 18; Jude 3; Eph. 1:17, 18; 3:10, 18*)

3. The Uniqueness and Universality of Christ

We affirm that there is only one Saviour and only one gospel, although there is a wide diversity of evangelistic approaches. We recognize that all men have some knowledge of God through his general revelation in nature. But we deny that this can save, for men suppress the truth by their unrighteousness. We also reject as derogatory to Christ and the gospel every kind of syncretism and dialogue which implies that Christ speaks equally through all religions and ideologies. Jesus Christ, being himself the only God-man, who gave himself as the only ransom for sinners, is the only mediator between God and man. There is no other name by which we must be saved. All men are perishing because of sin, but God loves all men, not wishing that any should perish but that all should repent. Yet those who reject Christ repudiate the joy of salvation and condemn themselves to eternal separation from God. To proclaim Jesus as "the Saviour of the world" is not to affirm that all men are either automatically or ultimately saved, still less to affirm that all religions offer salvation in Christ. Rather it is to proclaim God's love for a world of sinners and to invite all men to respond to him as Saviour and Lord in the wholehearted personal commit-

ment of repentance and faith. Jesus Christ has been exalted above
every other name; we long for the day when every knee shall bow
to him and every tongue shall confess him Lord. *(Gal. 1:6-9; Rom.
1:18-32; 1 Tim. 2:5, 6; Acts 4:12; Jn. 3:16-19; 2 Pet. 3:9; 2 Thes.
1:7-9; Jn. 4:42; Mt. 11:28; Eph. 1:20, 21; Phil. 2:9-11)*

4. The Nature of Evangelism

To evangelize is to spread the good news that Jesus Christ died
for our sins and was raised from the dead according to the Scriptures, and that as the reigning Lord he now offers the forgiveness
of sins and the liberating gift of the Spirit to all who repent and
believe. Our Christian presence in the world is indispensable to
evangelism, and so is that kind of dialogue whose purpose is to
listen sensitively in order to understand. But evangelism itself is
the proclamation of the historical, biblical Christ as Saviour and
Lord, with a view to persuading people to come to him personally
and so be reconciled to God. In issuing the gospel invitation we
have no liberty to conceal the cost of discipleship. Jesus still calls all
who would follow him to deny themselves, take up their cross, and
identify themselves with his new community. The results of evangelism include obedience to Christ, incorporation into his church,
and responsible service in the world. *(1 Cor. 15:3, 4; Acts 2:32-39;
Jn. 20:21; 1 Cor. 1:23; 2 Cor. 4, 5; 5:11, 20; Lk. 14:25-33;
Mk. 8:34; Acts 2:40, 47; Mk. 10:43-45)*

5. Christian Social Responsibility

We affirm that God is both the Creator and the Judge of all
men. We therefore should share his concern for justice and reconciliation throughout human society and for the liberation of men
from every kind of oppression. Because mankind is made in the
image of God, every person, regardless of race, religion, colour,
culture, class, sex or age, has an intrinsic dignity because of which
he should be respected and served, not exploited. Here too we
express penitence both for our neglect and for having sometimes
regarded evangelism and social concern as mutually exclusive. [Al-
though reconciliation with man is not reconciliation with God, nor
is social action evangelism, nor is political liberation salvation,
nevertheless we affirm that evangelism and sociopolitical involvement are both part of our Christian duty. For both are necessary

expressions of our doctrines of God and man, our love for our neighbour, and our obedience to Jesus Christ.] The message of salvation implies also a message of judgment upon every form of alienation, oppression, and discrimination, and we should not be afraid to denounce evil and injustice wherever they exist. When people receive Christ they are born again into his kingdom and must seek not only to exhibit but also to spread its righteousness in the midst of an unrighteous world. The salvation we claim should be transforming us in the totality of our personal and social responsibilities. Faith without works is dead. *(Acts 17:26, 31; Gen. 18:25; Is. 1:17; Ps. 45:7; Gen. 1:26, 27; Jas. 3:9; Lev. 19:18; Lk. 6:27, 35; Jas. 2:14-26; Jn. 3:3, 5; Mt. 5:20; 6:33; 2 Cor. 3:18; Jas. 2:20)*

6. *The Church and Evangelism*

We affirm that Christ sends his redeemed people into the world as the Father sent him, and that this calls for a similar deep and costly penetration of the world. We need to break out of our ecclesiastical ghettos and permeate non-Christian society. In the church's mission of sacrificial service evangelism is primary. World evangelization requires the whole church to take the whole gospel to the whole world. The church is at the very centre of God's cosmic purpose and is his appointed means of spreading the gospel. But a church which preaches the cross must itself be marked by the cross. It becomes a stumbling block to evangelism when it betrays the gospel or lacks a living faith in God, a genuine love for people, or scrupulous honesty in all things including promotion and finance. The church is the community of God's people rather than an institution, and must not be identified with any particular culture, social or political system, or human ideology. *(Jn. 17:18; 20:21; Mt. 28:19, 20; Acts 1:8; 20:27; Eph. 1:9, 10; 3:9-11; Gal. 6:14, 17; 2 Cor. 6:3, 4; 2 Tim. 2:19-21; Phil. 1:27)*

7. *Cooperation in Evangelism*

We affirm that the church's visible unity in truth is God's purpose. Evangelism also summons us to unity, because our oneness strengthens our witness, just as our disunity undermines our gospel of reconciliation. We recognize, however, that organizational unity may take many forms and does not necessarily forward evangelism. Yet we who share the same biblical faith should be closely

united in fellowship, work, and witness. We confess that our
testimony has sometimes been marred by sinful individualism and
needless duplication. We pledge ourselves to seek a deeper unity
in truth, worship, holiness, and mission. We urge the development
of regional and functional cooperation for the furtherance of the
church's mission, for strategic planning, for mutual encouragement, and for the sharing of resources and experience. *(Jn. 17:21,
23; Eph. 4:3, 4; Jn. 13:35; Phil. 1:27; Jn. 17:11-23)*

8. *Churches in Evangelistic Partnership*

We rejoice that a new missionary era has dawned. The
dominant role of Western missions is fast disappearing. God is raising up from the younger churches a great new resource for world
evangelization, and is thus demonstrating that the responsibility to
evangelize belongs to the whole body of Christ. All churches
should therefore be asking God and themselves what they should
be doing both to reach their own area and to send missionaries to
other parts of the world. A reevaluation of our missionary responsibility and role should be continuous. Thus a growing partnership
of churches will develop and the universal character of Christ's
church will be more clearly exhibited. We also thank God for
agencies which labour in Bible translation, theological education,
the mass media, Christian literature, evangelism, missions, church
renewal, and other specialist fields. They too should engage in
constant self-examination to evaluate their effectiveness as part of
the church's mission. *(Rom. 1:8; Phil. 1:5; 4:15; Acts 13:1-3;
I Thes. 1:6-8)*

9. *The Urgency of the Evangelistic Task*

More than 2,700 million people, which is more than two thirds
of mankind, have yet to be evangelized. We are ashamed that so
many have been neglected; it is a standing rebuke to us and to the
whole church. There is now, however, in many parts of the world
an unprecedented receptivity to the Lord Jesus Christ. We are
convinced that this is the time for churches and parachurch
agencies to pray earnestly for the salvation of the unreached and to
launch new efforts to achieve world evangelization. A reduction of
foreign missionaries and money in an evangelized country may
sometimes be necessary to facilitate the national church's growth

in self-reliance and to release resources for unevangelized areas. Missionaries should flow ever more freely from and to all six continents in a spirit of humble service. The goal should be, by all available means and at the earliest possible time, that every person will have the opportunity to hear, understand, and receive the good news. We cannot hope to attain this goal without sacrifice. All of us are shocked by the poverty of millions and disturbed by the injustices which cause it. Those of us who live in affluent circumstances accept our duty to develop a simple lifestyle in order to contribute more generously to both relief and evangelism. *(Jn. 9:4; Mt. 9:35-38; Rom. 9:1-3; 1 Cor. 9:19-23; Mk. 16:15; Is. 58:6, 7; Jas. 1:27; 2:1-9; Mt. 25:31-46; Acts 2:44, 45; 4:34, 35)*

10. *Evangelism and Culture*

The development of strategies for world evangelization calls for imaginative pioneering methods. Under God, the result will be the rise of churches deeply rooted in Christ and closely related to their culture. Culture must always be tested and judged by Scripture. Because man is God's creature, some of his culture is rich in beauty and goodness. Because he has fallen, all of it is tainted with sin and some of it is demonic. The gospel does not presuppose the superiority of any culture to another, but evaluates all cultures according to its own criteria of truth and righteousness, and insists on moral absolutes in every culture. Missions have all too frequently exported with the gospel an alien culture, and churches have sometimes been in bondage to culture rather than to the Scripture. Christ's evangelists must humbly seek to empty themselves of all but their personal authenticity in order to become the servants of others, and churches must seek to transform and enrich culture, all for the glory of God. *(Mk. 7:8, 9, 13; Gen. 4:21, 22; 1 Cor. 9:19-23; Phil. 2:5-7; 2 Cor. 4:5)*

11. *Education and Leadership*

We confess that we have sometimes pursued church growth at the expense of church depth, and divorced evangelism from Christian nurture. We also acknowledge that some of our missions have been too slow to equip and encourage national leaders to assume their rightful responsibilities. Yet we are committed to indigenous principles, and long that every church will have national leaders who manifest a Christian style of leadership in terms not of domination but of service. We recognize that there is a great need to improve theological education, especially for church leaders. In every nation and culture there should be an effective training programme for pastors and laymen in doctrine, discipleship, evangelism, nurture, and service. Such training programmes should not rely on any stereotyped methodology but should be developed by creative local initiatives according to biblical standards. *(Col. 1:27, 28; Acts 14:23; Tit. 1:5, 9; Mk. 10:42-45; Eph. 4:11, 12)*

12. Spiritual Conflict

We believe that we are engaged in constant spiritual warfare with the principalities and powers of evil, who are seeking to overthrow the church and frustrate its task of world evangelization. We know our need to equip ourselves with God's armour and to fight this battle with the spiritual weapons of truth and prayer. For we detect the activity of our enemy, not only in false ideologies outside the church, but also inside it in false gospels which twist Scripture and put man in the place of God. We need both watchfulness and discernment to safeguard the biblical gospel. We acknowledge that we ourselves are not immune to worldliness of thought and action, that is, to a surrender to secularism. For example, although careful studies of church growth, both numerical and spiritual, are right and valuable, we have sometimes neglected them. At other times, desirous to ensure a response to the gospel, we have compromised our message, manipulated our hearers through pressure techniques, and become unduly preoccupied with statistics or even dishonest in our use of them. All this is worldly. The church must be in the world; the world must not be in the church. *(Eph. 6:12; 2 Cor. 4:3, 4; Eph. 6:11, 13-18; 2 Cor. 10:3-5; 1 Jn. 2:18-26; 4:1-3; Gal. 1:6-9; 2 Cor. 2:17; 4:2; Jn. 17:15)*

13. Freedom and Persecution

It is the God-appointed duty of every government to secure conditions of peace, justice, and liberty in which the church may obey God, serve the Lord Christ, and preach the gospel without interference. We therefore pray for the leaders of the nations and call upon them to guarantee freedom of thought and conscience, and freedom to practise and propagate religion in accordance with the will of God and as set forth in The Universal Declaration of Human Rights. We also express our deep concern for all who have been unjustly imprisoned, and especially for our brethren who are suffering for their testimony to the Lord Jesus. We promise to pray and work for their freedom. At the same time we refuse to be intimidated by their fate. God helping us, we too will seek to stand against injustice and to remain faithful to the gospel, whatever the cost. We do not forget the warnings of Jesus that persecution is inevitable. *(1 Tim. 1:1-4; Acts 4:19; 5:29; Col. 3:24; Heb. 13:1-3; Lk. 4:18; Gal. 5:11; 6:12; Mt. 5:10-12; Jn. 15:18-21)*

14. *The Power of the Holy Spirit*

We believe in the power of the Holy Spirit. The Father sent his Spirit to bear witness to his Son; without his witness ours is futile. Conviction of sin, faith in Christ, new birth, and Christian growth are all his work. Further, the Holy Spirit is a missionary spirit; thus evangelism should arise spontaneously from a spirit-filled church. A church that is not a missionary church is contradicting itself and quenching the Spirit. Worldwide evangelization will become a realistic possibility only when the Spirit renews the church in truth and wisdom, faith, holiness, love, and power. We therefore call upon all Christians to pray for such a visitation of the sovereign Spirit of God that all his fruit may appear in all his people and that all his gifts may enrich the body of Christ. Only then will the whole church become a fit instrument in his hands, that the whole earth may hear his voice. *(1 Cor. 2:4; Jn. 15:26, 27, 16:8-11; 1 Cor. 12:3; Jn. 3:6-8; 2 Cor. 3:18; Jn. 7:37-39; 1 Thes. 5:19; Acts 1:8; Ps. 85:4-7; 67:1-3; Gal. 5:22, 23; 1 Cor. 12:4-31; Rom. 12:3-8)*

15. *The Return of Christ*

We believe that Jesus Christ will return personally and visibly, in power and glory, to consummate his salvation and his judgment. This promise of his coming is a further spur to our evangelism, for we remember his words that the gospel must first be preached to all nations. We believe that the interim period between Christ's ascension and return is to be filled with the mission of the people of God, who have no liberty to stop before the end. We also remember his warning that false Christs and false prophets will arise as precursors of the final antichrist. We therefore reject as a proud, self-confident dream the notion that man can ever build a utopia on earth. Our Christian confidence is that God will perfect his kingdom, and we look forward with eager anticipation to that day, and to the new heaven and earth in which righteousness will dwell and God will reign for ever. Meanwhile, we rededicate ourselves to the service of Christ and of men in joyful submission to his authority over the whole of our lives. *(Mk. 14:62; Heb. 9:28; Mk. 13:10; Acts 1:8-11; Mt. 28:20; Mk. 13:21-23; Jn. 2:18; 4:1-3; Lk. 12:32; Rev. 21:1-5; 2 Pet. 3:13; Mt. 28:18)*

Conclusion

Therefore, in the light of this our faith and our resolve, we enter into a solemn covenant with God and with each other, to pray, to plan, and to work together for the evangelization of the whole world. We call upon others to join us. May God help us by his grace and for his glory to be faithful to this our covenant! Amen, Alleluia!

Signed: _____

Date: _____

Issued at the International Congress on World Evangelization, Lausanne, Switzerland, July 1974. Used with permission of the Lausanne Committee for World Evangelization.

THE CHURCH TODAY
A Challenge to Popular Notions
(Hartford Appeal, 1975)

The renewal of Christian witness and mission requires constant examination of the assumptions shaping the church's life. Today an apparent loss of a sense of the transcendent is undermining the church's ability to address with clarity and courage the urgent tasks to which God calls it in the world. This loss is manifest in a number of pervasive themes. Many are superficially attractive, but upon closer examination we find these themes false and debilitating to the church's life and work. Among such themes are:

Theme 1: Modern thought is superior to all past forms of understanding reality, and is therefore normative for Christian faith and life.

In repudiating this theme we are protesting the captivity to the prevailing thought structures not only of the 20th century but of any historical period. We favor using any helpful means of understanding, ancient or modern, and insist that the Christian proclamation must be related to the idiom of the culture. At the same time, we affirm the need for Christian thought to confront and be confronted by all world-views, which are necessarily provisional.

Theme 2: Religious statements are totally independent of reasonable discourse.

The capitulation to the alleged primacy of modern thought takes two forms: one is the subordination of religious statements to the canons of scientific rationality; the other, equating reason with scientific rationality, would remove religious statements from the realm of reasonable discourse altogether. A religion of pure subjectivity and nonrationality results in treating faith statements as being, at best, statements about the believer. We repudiate both forms of capitulation.

Theme 3: Religious language refers to human experience and nothing else, God being humanity's noblest creation.

Religion is also a set of symbols and even of human projections. We repudiate the assumption that it is nothing but that. What is here at stake is nothing less than the reality of God: We did not invent God; God invented us.

Theme 4: Jesus can only be understood in terms of contemporary models of humanity.

This theme suggests a reversal of "the imitation of Christ"; that is, the image of Jesus is made to reflect cultural and counter-cultural notions of human excellence. We do not deny that all aspects of humanity are illumined by Jesus. Indeed, it is necessary to the universality of the Christ that he be perceived in relation to the particularities of the believers' world. We do repudiate the captivity to such metaphors, which are necessarily inadequate, relative, transitory, and frequently idolatrous. Jesus, together with the Scriptures and the whole of the Christian tradition, cannot be arbitrarily interpreted without reference to the history of which they are part. The danger is in the attempt to exploit the tradition without taking the tradition seriously.

Theme 5: All religions are equally valid; the choice among them is not a matter of conviction about truth but only of personal preference or lifestyle.

We affirm our common humanity. We affirm the importance of exploring and confronting all manifestations of the religious quest and of learning from the riches of other religions. But we repudiate this theme because it flattens diversities and ignores contradictions. In doing so, it not only obscures the meaning of Christian faith, but also fails to respect the integrity of other faiths. Truth matters; therefore differences among religions are deeply significant.

Theme 6: To realize one's potential and to be true to oneself is the whole meaning of salvation.

Salvation contains a promise of human fulfillment, but to identify salvation with human fulfillment can trivialize the promise. We affirm that salvation cannot be found apart from God.

Theme 7: Since what is human is good, evil can adequately be understood as failure to realize human potential.

This theme invites false understanding of the ambivalence of human existence and underestimates the pervasiveness of sin. Paradoxically, by minimizing the enormity of evil, it undermines serious and sustained attacks on particular social or individual evils.

Theme 8: The sole purpose of worship is to promote individual self-realization and human community.

Worship promotes individual and communal values, but it is above all a response to the reality of God and arises out of the fundamental need and desire to know, love, and adore God.

Theme 9: Institutions and historical traditions are oppressive and inimical to our being truly human; liberation from them is required for authentic existence and authentic religion.

Institutions and traditions are often oppressive. For this reason they must be subjected to relentless criticism. But human community inescapably requires institutions and traditions. Without them life would degenerate into chaos and new forms of bondage. The modern pursuit of liberation from all social and historical restraints is finally dehumanizing.

Theme 10: The world must set the agenda for the church. Social, political, and economic programs to improve the quality of life are ultimately normative for the church's missions in the world.

This theme cuts across the political and ideological spectrum. Its form remains the same, no matter whether the content is defined as upholding the values of the American way of life, promoting socialism, or raising human consciousness. The church must denounce oppressors, help liberate the oppressed, and seek to heal human misery. Sometimes the church's mission coincides with the world's programs. But the norms for the church's activity derive from its own perception of God's will for the world.

Theme 11: An emphasis on God's transcendence is at least a hindrance to, and perhaps incompatible with, Christian social concern and action.

This supposition leads some to denigrate God's transcendence. Others, holding to a false transcendence, withdraw into religious privatism or individualism and neglect the personal and communal responsibility of Christians for the earthly city. From a biblical perspective, it is precisely because of confidence in God's reign over all aspects of life that Christians must participate fully in the struggle against oppressive and dehumanizing structures and their manifestations in racism, war, and economic exploitation.

Theme 12: The struggle for a better humanity will bring about the kingdom of God.

The struggle for a better humanity is essential to Christian faith and can be informed and inspired by the biblical promise of the kingdom of God. But imperfect human beings cannot create a perfect society. The kingdom of God surpasses any conceivable utopia. God has his own designs, which confront ours, surprising us with judgment and redemption.

Theme 13: The question of hope beyond death is irrelevant or at best marginal to the Christian understanding of human fulfillment.

This is the final capitulation to modern thought. If death is the last word, then Christianity has nothing to say to the final questions of life. We believe that God raised Jesus from the dead and are "... convinced that there is nothing in death or life, in the realm of spirits or superhuman powers, in the world as it is or in the world as it shall be, in the forces of the universe, in heights or depths—nothing in all creation that can separate us from the love of God in Christ Jesus our Lord"

(*Romans 8:38f.*).

Reprinted from *Origins,* February 6, 1975, Vol. 4, No. 33, published by National Catholic News Service, 1312 Massachusetts, N.W., Washington, DC 20005.

BREAKING BARRIERS: NAIROBI 1975
Fifth Assembly of the World Council of Churches
November 23—December 10

Following are two excerpts from the 100-page report submitted by six working sections within the WCC organization. The first twenty points are from the section "Confessing Christ Today." The second statement is from the section on "Human Development: Ambiguities of Power, Technology, and Quality of Life." The complete text together with an introduction to Nairobi 1975 and the business of the Assembly is available in the book edited by David M. Paton, *Breaking Barriers: Nairobi 1975; the Official Report of the Fifth Assembly of The World Council of Churches, Nairobi, 23 November—10 December, 1975* (Grand Rapids: William B. Eerdmans, London: SPCK, 1976, and Geneva: World Council of Churches). Excerpted by permission.

Section I: Confessing Christ Today
Introduction

1. Today's world offers many political lords as well as secular and religious saviours. Nevertheless, as representatives of churches gathered together in the World Council of Churches, we boldly confess Christ alone as Saviour and Lord. We confidently trust in the power of the gospel to free and unite all children of God throughout the world.

2. Amid today's cries of anguish and shouts of oppression, we have been led by the Holy Spirit to confess Jesus Christ as our Divine Confessor. Confident in the Word of God of the holy Scriptures, we confess both our human weakness and our divine strength: "Since then we have a great high priest who has passed through the heavens, Jesus, the Son of God, let us hold fast our confession"

(Heb. 4:14).

3. As our high priest, Christ mediates God's new covenant through both salvation and service. Through the power of the cross, Christ promises God's righteousness and commands true justice. As the royal priesthood, Christians are therefore called to engage in both evangelism and social action. We are commissioned to proclaim the gospel of Christ to the ends of the earth. Simultaneously, we are commanded to struggle to realize God's will for peace, justice, and freedom throughout society.

4. In the same high priestly prayer which bids "that they may be one," Jesus also discloses the distinctive lifestyle of those who have been set apart to serve in the church's universal priesthood. While we are "not of" the world, even as he was not of the world, so we are also sent "into" the world, just as he was sent into the world (Jn. 17:16, 18).

5. Christians witness in word and deed to the inbreaking reign of God. We experience the power of the Holy Spirit to confess Christ in a life marked by both suffering and joy. Christ's decisive battle has been won at Easter, and we are baptized into his death that we might walk in newness of life (Rom. 6:4). Yet we must still battle daily against those already dethroned, but not yet destroyed, "principalities and powers" of this rebellious age. The Holy Spirit leads us into all truth, engrafting persons into the body of Christ in which all things are being restored by God.

6. Our life together is thereby committed to the costly discipleship of the church's divine confessor. His name is above every name: "that at the name of Jesus every knee should bow, in heaven and on earth and under the earth, and every tongue confess that Jesus Christ is Lord, to the glory of God the Father" (Phil. 2:10-11).

Confessing Christ as an Act of Conversion
The Christ of God

7. Jesus asks: "Who do you say that I am?" At the same time he calls us into discipleship: "If any man would come after me, let him deny himself and take up his cross and follow me" (Mt. 16:24). We confess Jesus as the Christ of God, the hope of the world, and commit ourselves to his will. Before we confess him, he confesses us, and in all our ways, he precedes us. We therefore confess with great joy:

8. Jesus Christ is the *one witness of God,* to whom we listen and witness as the incarnate Son of God in life and death (Jn. 14:8). "You are my witnesses.... I am the first and the last. There is no God except me" was said to Israel (Is. 43:8-11). So we are the witnesses of Christ and his kingdom to all people until the end of the world.

9. Jesus Christ is the *true witness of God* (Rev. 3:14). Into the world of lies, ambiguity, and idolatry, he brings "the truth that liberates" (Jn. 8:32). And as God has sent him, so he sends us.

10. Jesus Christ is the *faithful witness to God* (Rev. 1:5). In his self-offering on the cross he redeems us from sin and godless powers and reconciles creation with God. Therefore, we shall live for God and shall be saved in God. "There is no condemnation for those who are in Christ Jesus, who walk not after the flesh but after the Spirit" (Rom. 8:1ff).

11. We believe with certainty in the *presence and guidance of the Holy Spirit,* who proceeds from the Father and bears witness to Christ (Jn. 15:26). Our witness to Christ is made strong in the Holy Spirit and is alive in the confessing community of the church.

Our Discipleship, His Lordship

12. In our confessing Christ today and in our continuing conversion to the way of Christ, we encourage and support one another.

13. *Confessing Christ and being converted to his discipleship belong inseparably together.* Those who confess Jesus Christ deny themselves, their selfishness and slavery to the godless "principalities and powers," take up their crosses, and follow him. Without clear confession of Christ our discipleship cannot be recognized; without costly discipleship people will hesitate to believe our confession. The costs of discipleship—e.g., becoming a stranger among one's own people, being despised because of the gospel, persecuted because of resistance to oppressive powers, and imprisoned because of love for the poor and lost—are bearable in face of the costly love of God, revealed in the passion of Jesus.

14. We *deplore* cheap conversions, without consequences. We *deplore* a superficial gospel-preaching, an empty gospel without a call into personal and communal discipleship. We *confess* our own fear of suffering with Jesus. We are afraid of persecutions, fear,

and death. Yet, the more we look upon the crucified Christ alone and trust the power of the Holy Spirit, the more our anxiety is overcome. "When we suffer with him, we shall also be glorified with him" (Rom. 8:17). We revere the martyrs of all ages and of our time, and look to their example for courage.

15. We *deplore* conversions without witness to Christ. There are millions who have never heard the good news. We *confess* that we are often ashamed of the gospel. We find it more comfortable to remain in our own Christian circles than to witness in the world. The more we look upon our risen Lord, the more our indolence is overcome and we are enabled to confess: "Woe to me if I do not preach the gospel!" (1 Cor. 9:16).

16. We *deplore* also that our confessing Christ today is hindered by the different denominations, which split the confessing community of the church. We understand the confessions of faith of our different traditions as guidelines, not as substitutes, for our actual confessing in the face of today's challenges. Because being converted to Christ necessarily includes membership in the confessing body of Christ, we *long and strive* for a worldwide community.

17. *In confessing Christ and in being converted to his lordship, we experience the freedom of the Holy Spirit and express the ultimate hope for the world.* Through his true and faithful witness Jesus Christ has set us free from the slavery of sin to the glorious freedom of the Spirit. Within the vicious circle of sin, death, and the devil are the vicious circles of hunger, oppression, and violence. Likewise, liberation to justice, better community, and human dignity on earth is within the great freedom of the Spirit, who is nothing less than the power of the new creation.

18. We regret all divisions in thinking and practice between the personal and the corporate dimensions. "The whole gospel for the whole person and the whole world" means that we cannot leave any area of human life and suffering without the witness of hope.

19. We regret that some reduce liberation from sin and evil to social and political dimensions, just as we regret that others limit liberation to the private and eternal dimensions.

20. In the witness of our whole life and our confessing community we *work* with passionate love for the total liberation of the people and *anticipate* God's kingdom to come. We *pray* in the

freedom of the Spirit and *groan* with our suffering fellow human beings and the whole groaning creation until the glory of the triune God is revealed and God will be all in all. Come, Lord Jesus, come to us, come to the world!

o   o   o

Power and Justice

75. In order to make sure that the elitist and nonparticipatory structures which exist in society are not duplicated in the lifestyle, preaching, teaching, and decision-making of the churches, we call the churches to a serious self-criticism of their economic, political, and ideological role in their own societies. Moreover, we fraternally appeal to all churches to examine their interest in and concern for:

1. Social justice.
2. Peaceful coexistence of nations.
3. Participation in people's organizations.
4. Participation in an educational process which will develop critical awareness in order to begin to shape the features of a new society.

76. The present constellation of power requires a rethinking of the relationship between church and state as this was stated at the Oxford Conference, 1937. We therefore recommend the churches throughout the world to search for ways by which they may fully exercise their priestly and prophetic role and, at the same time, contribute to a more just and free society.

77. We witness with hope the increase of commitment to a more just and human society within many churches and Christian organizations all over the world. We recommend the churches and the WCC to continue to clarify and articulate the theological criteria of this engagement, taking into account recent regional experiences.

78. We request the churches to coordinate efforts with the WCC—through its appropriate subunits—in order to continue research and dialogue and to develop documentation on the role of the transnational corporations. In this sense we ask the WCC to aid the member churches to undertake or pursue this research at

local, national, and regional levels in order to enable people to participate in the shaping of a new economic order.

79. In view of the increasing worldwide trend to militarism which in itself is contrary to the Christian view of a world of justice and peace, and its tremendous negative impact in the process of development geared towards social justice, self-reliance, and economic growth, we strongly recommend that the churches and the WCC should make concrete the warnings they have already pronounced against militarism. We therefore recommend to the WCC to convene a special consultation on the nature of militarism as a preparation for a Programme to Combat Militarism.

Quality of Life

80. We call the attention of the churches to the growing concern over the consequences of modern science-based technological developments with their accompaniment of a deteriorating environment and debased and alienating forms of human communities. This has resulted in a new call to consider the "quality of life." This is an emphasis on the quality rather than the quantity of material things and on the obligation of the affluent both to provide basic necessities for all the people of planet Earth and to modify their own consumption patterns, so as to reduce their disproportionate and spiritually destructive drain on earth's nonrenewable and renewable resources, excessive use of energy resulting in contamination of the sea and air, and urban concentration and rural poverty that are breeding grounds of starvation, crime, and despair.

81. In solidarity with all who share our concern for quality of life, we encourage churches and Christians to take action to alter those structures and practices which hinder the achievement of an appropriate quality of life.

82. We ask all Christians to take costly and exemplary actions to show by deeds and words their solidarity with and concern for those who are deprived of adequate quality of life.

83. We urge Christians, individually and corporately, to pray for grace and courage to persist in the task of working obediently for the restoration of creation.

84. Recognizing that many groups are today engaged in a search for a new lifestyle which enhances quality of life, we urge

all Christians and churches to engage in a genuinely open dialogue with, and to support, such groups. It is important in this sense to be sensitive to meet lifestyles of the younger generations.

85. One of the main issues taken up by International Women's Year was the crucial contribution of women in relation to problems of development and quality of life. Issues of malnutrition, starvation, family size, etc., all these ultimately focus on what women do as overseers of the nutritional needs of their families and the education of their children. Therefore it is incumbent on the churches to take note of this and to see that women are included at all levels of decision-making regarding these critical and global issues that affect the work, education, legal rights, and contribution of women.

A Final Word

While the above recommendations are addressed to the member churches of the WCC, and also to the NCC itself, we hope that individuals, groups, and local congregations study and discuss these recommendations towards local involvement and appropriate action.

EVANGELIZATION IN THE MODERN WORLD

Apostolic Exhortation of Pope Paul VI

(December 8, 1975)

2. *What is Evangelization?*

A complex reality

17. In the church's evangelizing action there are elements and aspects which must always be respected. Some of them, in fact, are so important that they are, at times, taken as simply identical with evangelization. Thus, evangelization has been defined as the proclamation of Christ to those who do not know him or as preaching, catechizing, baptizing, and administering the other sacraments.

But no such partial and imperfect definition can do justice to the rich, complex, and dynamic reality we call evangelization. In fact, it risks impoverishing or even distorting it. For, evangelization cannot really be understood unless all its essential elements are taken into account.

These elements were emphasized by the Synod of Bishops and are now being more fully studied under the influence of the Synod's work. We are happy to see that the factors thus considered important are essentially the same as those insisted on by the Second Vatican Council in its Dogmatic Constitution on the Church, its Pastoral Constitution on the Church in the World of Today, and its Decree on the Missionary Activity of the Church.

Renewal of mankind

18. In the church's mind, to evangelize means to bring the good news to every sphere of the human, so that its influence may work within mankind to transform it: "See, I make all things new!"[1] But the human race cannot be renewed unless individual

209

men are first made new with the newness that flows from baptism[2] and a life according to the gospel.[3] The aim of evangelization is to bring about this interior change. If, then, we must attempt to summarize the meaning of evangelization, we will be more truthful and accurate in saying that the church evangelizes when she strives, solely by the divine power of the message she proclaims,[4] to transform the hearts of each and every man, along with their activities, their lives and their whole environment.

19. We spoke of transforming every sphere of the human. The church is not interested merely in preaching the gospel in ever wider geographical areas and to ever larger multitudes of men. She wishes to touch and transform, by the gospel's power, all the standards of judgment; the reigning values, the interests, the patterns of thinking, the motives, and ideals of mankind which are now in disaccord with God's Word and his plan of salvation.

Evangelization of cultures

20. We can put all this in other words and say that we must evangelize (not from outside, as though it were a matter of adding an ornament or a coat of paint, but from within, at the core and root of life), or imbue with the gospel, the cultures and culture of man, in the very broad and rich sense these terms have in the Pastoral Constitution on the Church in the World of Today.[5]

The gospel, and therefore evangelization as well, cannot be identified with any particular culture but it is independent of all cultures. On the other hand, the reign of God which the gospel proclaims takes concrete form in the lives of men who are profoundly shaped by their particular culture. It is also a fact that elements of man's culture and cultures must be used in building the kingdom of God. Therefore, although the gospel and evangelization do not properly belong to any culture, neither are they incompatible with any. On the contrary, they can enter into all of them without being subservient to any.

The separation between the gospel and culture is undoubtedly a sad fact of our age, as it has been of others. We must therefore be zealous and make every effort to evangelize man's culture or, more accurately, his cultures. These must achieve rebirth through encounter with the good news. This encounter will not take place, however, unless the good news is preached.

Primordial importance of the witness given by Christian life

21. The good news must be proclaimed first and foremost in the form of witness. See! There is a Christian, or a group of Christians, who, in the midst of the human community where they live their lives, show that they are able to understand and accept others, that they share the lives and fortunes of their fellowmen, and that they side with all who seek to defend what is good and noble. Moreover, simply and spontaneously they radiate their faith in spiritual values that are far superior to the ordinary values men accept and their hope in an invisible reality which even the most daring mind cannot imagine. Through silent witness such as this these Christians force those who observe them to ask questions: What makes these men what they are? Why do they live as they do? Who or what motivates them? Why do they live in our midst?

Such witness is already a wordless but powerful and effective proclamation of the good news and the beginning of an evangelization. The questions are perhaps the first that many non-Christians put to themselves, whether they be people to whom Christ has never been preached, or baptized people who do not live a Christian life, or men who live in a Christian society but are not Christian in their principles, or simply men who are painfully looking for something or Someone whose existence they sense but whom they cannot name. Other questions too, more profound and pressing, will be roused by this witnessing which is compounded of presence, sharing, and solidarity, and which is a necessary, and usually the first, stage in the process of evangelization.[6]

All Christians are called to give this witness and can, thereby, be authentic heralds of the gospel. We think here especially of the duty and responsibility countries have to the immigrants they receive.

Need of explicit proclamation

22. All this is not enough, however, since even the finest testimony will be ineffective in the long run unless it is illumined and justified (what Peter called giving "the reason for this hope of yours"[7]) and explained by a clear and unambiguous preaching of the Lord Jesus. The good news which is proclaimed through the witness of a life must sooner or later also be proclaimed through the word of life. There is no authentic evangelization unless the

name and teaching, the life and promises, the kingdom and mystery of Jesus the Nazarene, Son of God, are preached.

The whole history of the church, beginning with Peter's sermon on Pentecost, is inseparable from the history of its preaching. In every period of history the church has been constantly impelled by the ardent desire to evangelize and has known but one motivating concern: Whom shall we send to announce the mystery of Jesus? In what language is this mystery to be preached? How shall we make it reach and be understood by all who ought to hear it? This announcement—in kerygma, preaching, or catechesis—is so important a part of evangelization that it has often become a synonym for it. Yet, it is in fact but a part of the whole.

A vital commitment within a community

23. The reason for this is that the proclamation is not fully effective and meaningful unless it is heeded, accepted, and appropriated, and unless it leads to a wholehearted commitment on the part of the hearer. The commitment is undoubtedly to the truths a merciful God reveals but, far more importantly, it is to the kind of life (a life henceforth transformed) of which the truths speak.

In a word, a man commits himself to the reign of God, that is, to the "new world," the new state of things, the new manner of life in community, which the gospel brings into being. Such a commitment cannot abstract from real life but is shown by visible, tangible entry into the community of the faithful. Those who are converted enter a community that is of its nature a sign of new and transformed life. That community is the church, the visible sacrament of salvation.[8]

Entry into the community is in turn expressed in many other signs which prolong and explain the basic sign, which is the church herself. Because of the dynamism inherent in evangelization, he who accepts the gospel as the Word of life[9] will normally express his acceptance in sacramental signs, namely, commitment to the church and reception of the sacraments which manifest and support that commitment through the grace they bestow.

A new apostolate

24. Finally, the person who has been evangelized in turn evangelizes others. Here is the test of truth, the touchstone of evan-

gelization, for it is inconceivable that a man should have received God's Word and committed himself to God's reign and yet not bear witness to and proclaim the gospel.

Having made these observations on the meaning of evangelization, we must add one final point which we think will shed light on the reflections to follow.

Evangelization, we said, is a complex process with various aspects: renewal of mankind, witness, open proclamation, commitment of the heart, entry into the community, reception of the signs and apostolic action. These various elements may seem to conflict or even to be mutually exclusive. In fact, however, they complement and enrich one another. For this reason, each element must be seen in conjunction with the others. It was the merit of the recent Synod of Bishops that it so strongly urged us not to disjoin but to unite all the elements so that the total work of evangelization, as carried on by the church, might be fully understood. It is this comprehensive vision which we wish to unfold now as we consider the content of evangelization, the means used, those to whom it is directed, and those who are charged with it.

3. The Content of Evangelization
Essential content and secondary elements

25. There are certainly numerous elements of Christ's message which are secondary. The way these are presented depends a good deal on changing conditions and, consequently, the elements themselves change. But there is also an essential content, a vital substance, which cannot change or be passed over in silence without seriously distorting the very nature of evangelization.

26. It may not be superfluous to remind ourselves that to evangelize means, first and foremost, to bear direct and simple witness to the God whom Jesus Christ revealed in the Holy Spirit: witness that in his Son he loved the world and that in the incarnate Word he gave existence to all things and called men to eternal life. Such testimony about God will perhaps be for many a light shed on the unknown God[10] whom they adore without being able to name him or whom they seek by a hidden instinct of the heart after experiencing the emptiness of all the idols. But the testimony acquires its full evangelizing power when it shows that this Creator is not a nameless power far distant from man but is our Father. We

are "called the children of God," for "that is what we are!"[11] and we are, therefore, all brothers in God.

The central message

27. Evangelization will always have as the foundation, center, and supreme focus of its dynamism the clear proclamation that in Jesus Christ, the Son of God who became man, died and rose from the dead, salvation is offered to every man as a gracious gift inspired by God's mercy.[12] This is not a purely immanent salvation, measured by material or even spiritual needs which relate solely to man's temporal existence and can be wholly identified with his temporal desires, hopes, occupations, and struggles. No, it is a salvation which reaches far beyond these limited concerns and involves a communion with the sole Absolute, that is, with God. The salvation God offers us in Christ is, therefore, transcendent and eschatological; while it begins in this life, its culmination is in eternity.

28. Evangelization must, therefore, include a prophetic proclamation of another life or, to put it differently, of man's noblest and lasting vocation which is both continuous and discontinuous with his present state. This other life transcends time and history; it transcends the things of this world which is passing away, and the events of this world which have a hidden dimension which will someday be revealed to us; it even transcends man himself, whose true destiny cannot be realized in this temporal life but will be manifested in the life to come.[13]

Consequently, evangelization includes the preaching of hope in the promises God has made in the new covenant through Jesus Christ; the preaching of God's love for us and our love for God; the preaching of brotherly love for all men (an ability to give and forgive, to deny ourselves and help our brothers), a love that derives from love for God and is the very heart of the gospel; the preaching of the mystery of iniquity and of the active search for the good. It includes the always necessary preaching of the quest for God himself through prayer, especially of adoration and thanksgiving, but also through communion with the visible sign of union with God, namely, the church of Jesus Christ. This communion is, in turn, manifested through the use of the sacraments, those other signs of the Christ who lives and acts in the church. To

celebrate the sacraments in such a fashion that they become a celebration of the real fullness of Christian life is not—as is sometimes
falsely said, even today—to put an obstacle in the way of, or
deviate from, true evangelization but rather to bring evangelization to its completion. For, evangelization in its fullest form means
not only the proclamation of a message but the building up of the
church, and the church cannot live without the life breath which is
assured her by the sacramental life which culminates in the Eucharist.[14]

29. Evangelization cannot be complete, however, unless account is taken of the reciprocal links between the gospel and the
concrete personal and social life of man. For this reason evangelization requires a message which is explicit, adapted to varying
situations, and constantly related to the rights and obligations of
each individual, to family life without which the development of
the individual becomes extremely difficult,[15] to common life in society, to international life, and to peace, justice, and development.
Finally, it must be a message, especially strong and pointed today,
of liberation.

30. Everyone is aware of the manner in which numerous
bishops from all continents, but especially from the Third World,
spoke on the subject of liberation at the recent Synod. They spoke
with pastoral fervor and with pastoral accents which echoed the
voices of those millions of faithful who belong to the peoples of the
Third World. These peoples, as we know, are striving with all their
might to overcome the conditions which force them to live such a
marginal life: hunger, chronic illnesses, illiteracy, penury, injustice
at the international level and especially in commercial relations,
and economic and cultural neocolonialism which is sometimes as
cruel as political colonialism. The church has the duty, as her
bishops have insisted, of proclaiming the liberation of millions of
human beings, many of whom are her children. She also has the
duty of helping the process of liberation get underway, of testify-
ing in its behalf, and of working for its completion. All this is by no
means unrelated to evangelization.

Evangelization and the advancement of man

31. There are close links between evangelization and the advancement, or liberation and development, of man. The links are

anthropological, inasmuch as the human being to be evangelized is not an abstraction but is subject to social and economic conditions. The links are also theological, because the plan of creation cannot be dissociated from the plan of redemption which aims at overcoming injustice and restoring justice in very concrete ways. The links are eminently evangelical, which is to say that they belong to the order of love. How can the new commandment be preached unless the real, authentic development of man is fostered through the creation of justice and peace? It was this which we wished to emphasize when we insisted that evangelization neither "could [nor] should ignore the importance of . . . current problems concerning justice, liberation, development, and world peace. This would mean forgetting the gospel lesson about love for our suffering, needy neighbor."[16]

The same bishops who zealously, prudently, and courageously took up this serious problem at the Synod also provided, to our great joy, luminously clear principles for grasping the significance and deeper meaning of the liberation which Jesus of Nazareth proclaimed and made a reality and which the church preaches.

No reduction or ambiguity

32. It cannot be denied that many Christians, generous people who are concerned about the serious questions liberation raises and who want to involve the church in the liberation movement, think of the church's mission as purely temporal and try to limit it accordingly.

They interpret her functions according to an anthropological scheme, identify the salvation she preaches with material prosperity, and would have her restrict herself to political or social action without any concern for the spiritual or the religious.

But, if this were a true picture of the church, she would have lost her essential meaning. Her message of liberation would be radically altered and could easily be twisted and distorted to serve ideological systems and political parties. She would be stripped of all authority to preach liberation as God's representative. It was for this reason that in our address, cited just above, at the opening of the Third Synod of Bishops, we insisted on "the need to restate clearly the specifically religious aim of evangelization. It would lose all its significance if it were to diverge from the religious fulcrum which sustains it: the kingdom of God ... in its fully theological meaning."[17]

Liberation according to the gospel

33. We must rather, therefore, say the following about the liberation which evangelization proclaims and endeavors to bring about:

(a) It cannot be limited purely and simply to the economic, social, or cultural spheres but must concern the whole man in all his dimensions, including his relation to an "absolute" and even to *the* Absolute, which is God.

(b) It is based, therefore, on a conception of man, an anthropology, which can never be sacrificed to the requirements of some strategy or other, or to practice, or to short-term effectiveness.

34. Consequently, in proclaiming liberation and ranging herself with all who toil and suffer for it, the church cannot allow herself or her mission to be limited to the purely religious sphere while she ignores the temporal problems of man. At the same time, however, she reaffirms the primacy of her spiritual role, refuses to replace the proclamation of God's reign with the preaching of various purely human liberations, and insists that even her contribution to liberation is incomplete and imperfect if she fails to preach salvation in Jesus Christ.

And on an evangelical vision of man

35. The church connects but never equates human liberation with salvation in Jesus Christ. For, she knows from divine revelation, historical experience, and reflection on the faith that not every concept of liberation is necessarily consistent with the gospel vision of man, things, and events. She knows that the acquisition of liberation, prosperity, and development is not enough to bring about the reign of God.

The church is, moreover, thoroughly convinced that any temporal or political liberation contains within itself the seeds of its own negation and must fail to achieve the lofty ideal it sets itself. For, its true motive is not the establishment of justice in charity, and its driving passion is not spiritual virtue or the winning of eternal salvation and blessedness in God as a final goal. None of this is changed by the fact that the liberation movement tries to justify itself by one or the other passages of the Old and New Testaments; that it thinks its theoretical postulates and norms of action are supported by theological principles and conclusions; or that it believes itself to be the theology for our times.   . .

Conversion is needed

36. The church certainly considers it highly important to establish structures which are more human, more just, more respectful of the rights of the person, less oppressive and coercive. She knows, however, that even the most perfect structures and the most ideal systems quickly become inhuman unless the inhuman bent of man's heart is corrected, unless those who live in or control these structures are converted in heart and mind.

37. The church cannot accept violence, especially military (uncontrollable once unleashed), or even the death of a single man as the way to liberation. She knows that violence always begets violence and necessarily leads to new forms of oppression and of servitude even more bitter than the one from which man was to be liberated. We said this in plain words during our sojourn in Colombia: "Allow us, finally, to exhort you not to place your trust in violence and revolution. That is contrary to the Christian spirit, and can even delay, rather than advance, that social uplifting to which you lawfully aspire."[18] And again: "We must say and reaffirm that violence is not in accord with the gospel, that it is not Christian; and that sudden or violent changes of structures would be deceitful, would be ineffective of themselves, and certainly would not be in conformity with the dignity of the people."[19]

Specific contribution of the church

38. Having said this, we must also say how happy we are that the church is becoming ever more conscious of the true and wholly evangelical way in which she is to collaborate in the liberation of man. And what is her role? She strives increasingly to arouse numerous Christians to devote themselves to the liberation of their fellows. She offers these Christian "liberators" the spirit and guidance of faith, the motivation of brotherly love, and a social doctrine which no authentic Christian can fail to heed but must rather make the basis of his own experiential wisdom so as to derive from that teaching principles for action, participation, and

duty. All this—faith, love, social doctrine—has nothing to do with clever tactics or service to a political party, but should be characteristic of every Christian in his zealous efforts. The church constantly strives to link the Christian struggle for liberation with the comprehensive plan of salvation which she proclaims.

What we have just been saying was said a number of times in the discussions at the Synod. In addition, in order that there might be even greater clarity on the subject, we spoke of it in our address to the fathers at the close of the Synod.[20]

We hope that these various considerations will eliminate the ambiguities which the word "liberation" too often has when used by ideological systems and political parties. The liberation which evangelization preaches and for which it prepares the way is the liberation Christ himself preached and bestowed upon us through his sacrifice.

Religious liberty

39. The legitimate liberation which is connected with evangelization and seeks structures protective of human freedom is inseparable from the defense of the basic rights of man, among which religious liberty holds an important place. We recently spoke on this urgent question and observed, "How many Christians, even today, simply because they are Christians, simply because they are Catholics, live under the burden of systematic oppression! The drama of fidelity and religious freedom still goes on, even if they are hidden behind categorical statements in favor of the rights of persons and human society!"[21]

Notes

1. Rev. 21:5; see 2 Cor. 5:17; Gal. 6:15.

2. See Rom. 6:4.

3. See Eph. 4:23-24; Col. 3:9-10.

4. See Rom. 1:16; 1 Cor. 1:18; 2:4.

5. No. 53: AAS 58 (1966) 1075 [TPS XI, 295].

6. See Tertullian, *Apologeticum*, 39: CCL 1, pp. 150-153; Minucius Felix, *Octavius*, 9 and 31: CSLP (Turin, 1963), pp. 11-13, 47-48.

7. 1 Pet. 3:15.

8. See Vatican II, *Dogmatic Constitution on the Church*, nos. 1, 9, 48: AAS 57 (1965) 5, 12-14, 53-54 [TPS X, 359, 364-365, 391-392]; *Pastoral Constitution on the*

Church in the World of Today, nos. 42, 45: AAS 58 (1966) 1060-1061 [TPS XI, 284-285, 288-289]; *Decree on the Missionary Activity of the Church*, nos. 1, 5: AAS 58 (1966) 947, 951-952 [TPS XI, 409, 413-414].

9. See Rom. 1:16; 1 Cor. 1:8.

10. See Acts 17:22-23.

11. 1 Jn. 3:1; see Rom. 8:14-17.

12. See Eph. 2:8; Rom. 1:16; Declaration of the Sacred Congregation for the Doctrine of the Faith, *Safeguarding Basic Christian Beliefs* (February 21, 1972): AAS 64 (1972) 237-241 [TPS XVII, 64-68].

13. See 1 Jn. 3:2; Rom. 8:29; Phil. 3:10-21; Vatican II, *Dogmatic Constitution on the Church*, nos. 48-51: AAS 57 (1965) 53-58 [TPS X, 391-394].

14. See the Declaration of the Sacred Congregation for the Doctrine of the Faith, *In Defense of Catholic Doctrine on the Church* (June 24, 1973): AAS 65 (1973) 396-408 [TPS XVIII, 145-157].

15. See Vatican II, *Pastoral Constitution on the Church in the World of Today*, nos. 47-52: AAS 58 (1966) 1067-1074 [TPS XI, 289-295]; Paul VI, Encyclical *Humanae Vitae:* AAS 60 (1968) 481-505 [TPS XIII, 329-346].

16. Paul VI, *Opening Address at the First Session of the Third Synod of Bishops* (September 27, 1974): AAS 66 (1974) 562 [TPS XIX, 189-190].

17. Paul VI, *Opening Address . . . ibid.* [TPS XIX, 189].

18. Paul VI, *Address to the "Campesinos" of Colombia* (August 23, 1968): AAS 60 (1968) 623 [TPS XIII, 236].

19. Paul VI, *Address on "Development Day" at Bogotá* (August 23, 1968): AAS 60 (1968) 627 [TPS XIII, 240]. See St. Augustine, *Epistola* 229, 2: PL 33:1020.

20. Paul VI, *Closing Address to the Third Synod of Bishops* (October 26, 1974): AAS 66 (1974) 637 [TPS XIX, 197].

21. Paul VI, *Address to a General Audience* (October 15, 1975): OR, October 17, 1975 [TPS XXI, 74].

Reprinted by permission of *Our Sunday Visitor* from *The Pope Speaks* 21, 1 (Spring, 1976), parts II and III, pp. 13-21. The full text (pp. 4-51) merits careful reading, thought, and discussion.

THE BOSTON AFFIRMATIONS
(January 6, 1976)

•The living God is active in current struggles to bring a reign of justice, righteousness, love, and peace.

•The Judeo-Christian traditions are pertinent to the dilemmas of our world.

•All believers are called to preach the good news to the poor, to proclaim release to the captives and recovery of sight to the blind, to set at liberty those who are oppressed, and to proclaim the acceptable year of the Lord.

Yet we are concerned about what we discern to be present trends in our churches, in religious thought, and in our society.

We see struggles in every arena of human life, but in too many parts of the church and theology we find retreat from these struggles.

Still, we are not without hope nor warrants for our hope. Hopeful participation in these struggles is at once action in faith, the primary occasion for personal spiritual growth, the development of viable structures for the common life, and the vocation of the people of God.

To sustain such participation, we have searched the past and the present to find the signs of God's future and of ours.

Thus, we make the following

AFFIRMATIONS:

Creation:
God Brings into Being All Resources,
　　All Life,
　　　　All Genuine Meanings.

Humanity is of one source
and is not ultimately governed by nature or history,
　　by the fabric of societies
　　　　or the depths of the self,
　　by knowledge
　　　　or belief.

God's triune activity sustains creative order,
　　evokes personal identity,
　　　　and is embodied in the dynamic movements
　　　　　　of human history
　　in an ever more inclusive community
　　　　of persons responsibly engaged
　　　　　　in all aspects
　　of the ecosphere, history, and thought.

Fall:
Humanity Is Estranged from the Source of Life.
We try to ignore or transcend the source and end
　　of life.
Or we try to place God in a transcendent realm
　　divorced from life.
Thereby we give license to domination,
　　indulgence,
　　　　pretense,
　　　　　　triviality,
　　　　　　　　and evasion.

We endanger creative order,

We destroy personal identity,

And we corrupt inspirited communities.

We allow tyranny, anarchy, and death to dominate the gift of life.

Exodus and Covenant:
God Delivers from Oppression and Chaos.
God Chooses Strangers, Servants,
    and Outcasts
to Be Witnesses and to Become a Community
of Righteousness and Mercy.

Beyond domination and conflict
God hears the cry of the oppressed
and works vindication for all.

God forms "nobodies" into a people of "somebodies" and makes known the laws of life.

The liberation experience calls forth celebrative response, demands responsibility in community, and opens people and nations for a common global history.

Prophecy:
In Compassion God Speaks to the Human Community Through Prophets.

Those who authentically represent God have interpreted—
    and will interpret—
the activity of God in social history.

They announce the presence of God in the midst of political and economic life;

They foretell the judgment and hope that are implicit in the
  loyalties and practices of the common life;

And they set forth the vision of covenantal renewal.

Wisdom:
*The Cultural Insights and Memories
of Many Peoples and Ages
Illuminate the Human Condition.*

The experience and lore of all cultures and groups bear within
  them values that are of wider meaning.

Racism,
Genocide,
Imperialism,
Sexism
  are thus contrary to God's purposes and impoverish us all.

Yet all wisdom must also be tested for its capacity to reveal the
  human dependence on the source of life,
to grasp the depths of sin,
to liberate,
to evoke prophecy,
and to form genuine covenant.

The New Covenant:
God Is Known to Us in Jesus Christ.
The source and end of life is disclosed in that suffering love
which breaks the power of sin and death,
which renders hope in the action of God to reconcile and
  transform the world,
which shatters the barriers of ethnic,
  class,
    familial,
      national
        and caste restrictions.
Meaning and divine activity are incarnate in history and human
  particularity.

Church Traditions:
God Calls Those Who Trust the Power of Suffering
Love
to Form into Communities of Celebration, Care, and
Involvement.
Those called together enact renewing forms of association and
movement to the ends of the earth,
responding by word and deed to the implications of faith for each
age and for us today:

—The early Eastern church celebrated the dependence of humanity
upon the cosmos,
and of the cosmos upon God,
demanding a sacramental attitude toward the whole of creation.

—The Formers of doctrine set forth the meanings of faith in the
face of cultured despisers,
exposed the frail foundations of various secularisms,
and gave new directions to both the faithful and civilization.

—The Monastics assumed vows to exemplify lifestyles beyond
preoccupation with gain, freedom from familial and sexual
stereotyping, and disciplined lives of service.

—The Scholastics engaged secular culture, demanding of each
generation critical and synthetic reappropriation of tradition.

—The Reformers preached the word of protest against religious
pretense and demanded reliance upon the gifts of divine empowerment.

—The Sectarians nurtured the spirit that cannot be contained by
priesthood, dogma, hierarchy, authoritative word, or any established power, and demanded
democracy,
freedom,
toleration,
and the redistribution of authority, power, and wealth.

—And today many reach out for wider fellowships, demanding ecumenical engagements and a witness which frees and unites.

Wherever the heirs of these movements are authentic,
    they confess their sins,
    worship the power that sustains them,
    form a company of the committed,
and struggle for justice and love against the powers and princi-
    palities of evil.

Present Witnesses:
The question today is
Whether the Heritage of This Past
Can Be Sustained, Preserved, and Extended
into the Future.

Society as presently structured,
Piety as presently practiced,
and
The churches as presently preoccupied
evoke
profound doubts about the prospects.

> *Yet We Are Surrounded by*
> *a Cloud of Witnesses Who*
> *Prophetically Exemplify or Discern*
> *The Activity of God.*

> *The Transforming Reality of God's Reign*
> *Is Found Today:*

—In the struggles of the poor to gain a share of the world's wealth,
to become creative participants in the common economic life,
and to move our world toward an economic democracy of equity
and accountability.

—In the transforming drive for ethnic dignity against the persistent
    racism of human hearts

and
social institutions.

—In the endeavor by women to overcome sexist subordination in
    the church's ministry, in society at large,
and in the images that bind our minds and bodies.

—In the attempts within families to overcome prideful domina-
    tion and degrading passivity and
to establish genuine covenants of mutuality and joyous fidelity.

—In the efforts by many groups to develop for modern humanity
    a love for its cities as centers of civility, culture, and human
    interdependence.

—In the demands of the sick and the elderly for inexpensive, accessible
    health care administered with concern,
    advised consent,
    and sensitivity.

—In the voices of citizens and political leaders who demand
    honesty and openness,
who challenge the misplaced trust of the nation in might,
and who resist the temptations to make a nation and its institutions
    objects of religious loyalty.

—In the research of science when it warns of dangers to humanity
and quests for those forms of technology which can sustain human
    well-being and preserve ecological resources.

—In the humanities and social sciences when the depths of human
    meanings are opened to inquiry and are allowed to open our
    horizons,
especially whenever there is protest against the subordination of
    religion to scientistic rationality
or against the removal of religion from realms of rational discourse.

—In the arts where beauty and meaning are explored, lifted up, and represented in ways that call us to deeper sensibilities.

—In the halls of justice when righteousness is touched with mercy,
when the prisoner and the wrongdoer are treated with dignity and
fairness.

—And especially in those branches and divisions of the church
where the truth is spoken in love,
where transforming social commitments are nurtured and persons
are brought to informed conviction,
where piety is renewed and recast in concert with the heritage,
and where such struggles as those here identified are seen as the
action of the living God who alone is worshiped.

ON THESE GROUNDS:

We cannot stand with those secular cynics and religious spiri-
tualizers
who see in such witnesses no theology, no eschatological urgency, and no Godly promise or judgment.
In such spiritual blindness, secular or religious, the world as God's
creation is abandoned,
sin rules,
liberation is frustrated,
covenant is broken,
prophecy is stilled,
wisdom is betrayed,
suffering love is transformed into triviality,
and the church is transmuted into a club for
self- or transcendental-awareness.

The Struggle Is Now Joined
for the Future of faith and
the Common Life.

We Call All Who Believe in the Living God
To Affirm,
To Sustain
and to Extend These Witnesses.

The following members of the Boston Industrial Mission Task Force participated, with some variation of regularity, in the process of drafting this statement.

Norman Faramelli   Max Stackhouse
Constance Parvey   Harvey Cox
Scott Paradise   Joseph Williamson
Mary Roodkowsky   George Rupp
Paul Santmire   David Dodson Gray
Richard Snyder   Elizabeth Dodson Gray
Jeanne Gallo   Ignacio Casteura
Moises Mendez   Robert Starbuck
John Snow   Eleanor McLaughlin
Preston Williams   Mary Hennessey
                                Jerry Handspicker

Reprinted by permission of Max L. Stackhouse, Andover Newton Theological School.

EVANGELISM TODAY
A Policy Statement of the National Council of the Churches of Christ in the United States of America

(Adopted by the Governing Board March 3, 1976)

Introductory Statement

This is a statement that was developed by the working group on evangelism of the Division of Church and Society, and expresses a common ground where representatives of a wide range of churches could meet with those who are members of the National Council of Churches. It is not intended as a comprehensive theological treatise on evangelism, but as a corrective to the recent dichotomy between "personal" evangelism and "social action." It is a description of a past and present pilgrimage and so does not attempt to address the problems yet to be encountered.

One way of setting forth what evangelism means in the ecumenical experience today is to review the journey of the past twenty-five years of that experience—a period in which evangelism has been a central issue in American church life. During this period of changing concepts of evangelism, its fullness has never been totally disclosed at any one time or place, and this statement does not attempt a final or definitive description of it.

In the 1950s, two major methods were utilized in evangelism: mass meeting campaigns and lay visitation programs, both inviting persons to make decisions for Jesus Christ. Although other factors probably contributed, these modes of sharing the gospel coincided in the 1950s with a season of growth in church membership unparalleled in American church history.

However, growth in church membership and calling people to Christian discipleship were not necessarily the same. In the early 1960s it became apparent that for many people joining the church had not produced a significant change of attitude or behavior. This failure of new church members to be enlisted in a pilgrimage toward fuller Christian discipleship called into question the effectiveness of the methods then being used. There followed an intense theological reexamination of what the demands of Christian discipleship should mean both for individuals and for society.

In the process of that reexamination, the practice of evangelism as a congregational function in which people are confronted with the gospel and called to Christian discipleship was minimized in those denominations which were working together in the National Council of Churches. Denominational attention was focused on social injustices, and efforts were made to mobilize church members to help rectify them. A false division resulted. Instead of social awareness and action being seen as natural expressions of Christian discipleship to which people are called by evangelism, social action was thought to be a contrast and corrective to evangelism. In this mistaken polarization between them both—and the whole life of the church—were weakened.

Today we can see the futility of that polarization, but the churches still seem strangely bound by a reluctance to name the name of Jesus as Lord and Savior. Christians seem to lack the facility today to exclaim with excitement, "Jesus loves me; therefore, I love you!" At this moment in history, there is a great need for the churches to recover the ability to name the name of Jesus Christ as Lord and Savior and to bear witness to that name in word and deed.

But naming the name and bearing witness to it must be better understood: commitment to Jesus Christ is a profound event. It is a *personal* event; by the power of the Holy Spirit sinners experience the divine forgiveness and commit themselves to live obediently to Christ the living Lord. It is a *social* event; relationships with friends, neighbors, and family are radically altered by the revolutionary demands and allowances of divine love. It is a *community* event; it engrafts one into the community of believers, the church. It is a *public* event; new confrontations with the institutions of society occur, for the "principalities and powers" which impoverish and enslave humanity cannot go unchallenged by Christians!

Commitment to Jesus Christ must be made in the context of the issues posed for us by the moment of history in which we find ourselves—history in which God is at work, through us and sometimes in spite of us. That commitment to Jesus Christ must have an impact on the issues of social and economic justice through the stewardship, integrity, and interdependence of Christian disciples. Thereby commitment to Jesus Christ is inescapably a personal, social, community, and public historical event which affects the world and the human beings in it for whom Christ died.

Commitment to Jesus Christ is not a once-for-all event. It is the beginning of one's spiritual pilgrimage of discipleship. Those who are disciples of Christ face continual turning-points which offer new experiences rooted in being "born anew to a living hope." We never move beyond the need to hear the renewing call to "repent and believe in the gospel," in order to live more obediently to the Word of the Lord in every area of life, turning from the dead values of self-centered living, acquisitive consumption, and upward social striving.

Commitment to Jesus Christ means to embrace more completely in our *personal* lives the new way of life which God's grace initiates, manifesting the Spirit's fruit of love, joy, peace, goodness, meekness, gentleness, and self-control. Commitment to Jesus Christ means in our *social* life to love others more deeply, even as Christ loves us and gave himself for us, a love which is giving, accepting, forgiving, seeking and helping. Commitment to Jesus Christ in *community* life means to be called out from the isolation of individualism, from conformity to the ways of the world into the fellowship of disciples which is the church, where by obedience we discover freedom, by humble service we are fulfilled, by sharing the suffering of others we are made whole. Commitment to Jesus Christ in our *public* lives means to be engaged more earnestly in the work not only of relieving the poor and hungry but removing the causes of poverty and hunger in the struggle to remedy both inequities and iniquities, in the liberation of the oppressed and the vindication of the deprived, in the establishment of God's rule in the affairs of humanity. Commitment to Jesus Christ brings confidence that, however dark the present hour, the ultimate victory is assured through him who is the Lord.

The task of evangelism today is calling people to repentance, to faith in Jesus Christ, to study God's Word, to continue steadfast in prayer, and to bearing witness to him. This is a primary function of the church in its congregational, denominational, and ecumenical manifestations. It challenges the most creative capabilities in the churches while at the same time depending upon the Holy Spirit to be the real evangelist.

Now, after the journey of the past twenty-five years, we can call upon people to confess the name of Jesus Christ and to bear witness to that name in their lives with a fuller understanding of Christian discipleship and a deeper commitment to share the good news we have found.

Reprinted by permission of Dean M. Kelley, National Council of Churches.

WORLD EVANGELISATION

Signs of Convergence and Divergence in Christian Understanding

John Stott

The evangelisation of the world has been the preoccupation of several Christian conferences in the middle 1970s. In January 1973 the Bangkok Assembly of the Commission on World Mission and Evangelism was entitled "Salvation Today." In July 1974 the evangelical International Congress on World Evangelisation produced the Lausanne Covenant. Later the same year the Third General Assembly of the Roman Catholic Synod of Bishops in Rome gave their attention to this topic. At Nairobi in November-December 1975 two sections of the Fifth Assembly of the World Council of Churches handled aspects of the subject, the first "Confessing Christ Today" and the third "Seeking Community: the common search of people of various faiths, cultures and ideologies." Then on December 8 1975, two days before the conclusion of the Nairobi Assembly, and in response to a request by the Roman Catholic Synod of Bishops, Pope Paul issued *Evangelii Nuntiandi,* his apostolic exhortation on "Evangelisation in the Modern World."

Reporting to the WCC Assembly at Nairobi, Dr. M. M. Thomas, moderator of the Central Committee of the WCC, devoted a third of his time to "the concept of evangelism in the modern world." Although he was speaking before the Pope's exhortation had been published, he drew attention to the conferences on evangelism in Bangkok, Lausanne, and Rome, as well as to the Orthodox Consultation "Confessing Christ Today" at Bucharest in 1974. He began by saying that "their theological convergence is very striking," and then went on to consider "the remaining divergences in our concept of evangelism." Now that the pope's exhortation and the Nairobi Report have been published, it is possible yet more fully to compare the current evangelical, ecumenical and Roman Catholic concepts of world evangelisation.

Although the Roman Catholic *Evangelii Nuntiandi* says little about the principalities and powers of darkness, its final section stresses that "evangelisation will never be possible without the action of the Holy Spirit." For it is he who not only gives his people an understanding of the gospel and the words to say, but also "predisposes the soul of the hearer to be open and receptive to the good news." Therefore, although "techniques of evangelisation are good," they "could not replace the gentle action of the Spirit." Without him the work of the evangeliser is impotent and valueless (75). Therefore, the pope in the Roman Catholic *Evangelii Nuntiandi* exhorts all evangelisers "to pray without ceasing to the Holy Spirit with faith and fervour, and to let themselves prudently be guided by him" (75).

But the relation between the present and the future is not worked out in the Roman Catholic document or indeed in the other two. Dr. M. M. Thomas spoke, in his Moderator's Report to the WCC, of the common ground between us in "the recognition of the eschatological basis for historical action." He also warned us of opposite dangers, on the one hand of a utopianism born of self-confidence, and on the other of an antiutopianism born of either laziness or unbelief. A clarification of the precise relationship between historical action and eschatological hope is greatly needed.

The accompanying chart tabulates "Ten Affirmations on Evangelism" from the Lausanne Covenant, *Evangelii Nuntiandi*, and Nairobi 75 as the basis of discussion on whether there is sufficient agreement for united evangelical activity. Despite the remaining divergences (which have to be raised at some point and faced with integrity) we still have to ask: Do the reports contain a sufficient measure of convergence to warrant some form of common witness? These affirmations are an attempt to sketch apparent areas of convergence and form a basis on which to discuss whether we agree enough to work together.

TEN AFFIRMATIONS ON EVANGELISM

1 The church is sent into the world	2 The church's mission in the world includes evangelism and social action	3 The content of the gospel is derived from the Bible	4 The gospel centres on Christ crucified and risen	5 Salvation is offered to sinners in the gospel through Jesus Christ
Christ sends his church into the world as he was himself sent into the world. Whenever the church withdraws from the world it denies an essential part of its nature and calling.	*The church's mission in the world comprises both evangelism and social action, while evangelism always remains a priority concern.*	*Evangelism is in essence the spread of the evangel, and this has been revealed to us in Holy Scripture.*	*The heart of the good news is Jesus Christ himself, who died for our sins on the cross and was then raised from the dead as the beginning of God's new creation*	*Through the death and resurrection of Jesus Christ God offers us salvation, or liberation from sin and death. God also wills liberation from social injustice. But the two must not be confused.*
Lausanne Covenant: God . . . has been calling out from the world a people for himself, and sending his people back into the world to be his servants and his witnesses (1).	We affirm that evangelism and socio political involvement are both part of our Christian duty (5). In the church's mission of sacrificial service evangelism is primary (6).	To evangelise is to spread the good news. . . . Evangelism is the proclamation of the historical, biblical Christ (4).	To evangelise is to spread the good news that Jesus Christ died for our sins and was raised from the dead (4).	Christ . . . as the reigning Lord . . . now offers the forgiveness of sins and the liberating gift of the Spirit (4). We . . . should share his (sc. God's) concern for . . . the liberation of m:n from every kind of oppression . . . although . . . political liberation (is not) salvation (5).

236

Evangelii Nuntiandi: Having been born consequently out of being sent, the church in her turn is sent by Jesus. ... For the Christian community is never closed in upon itself (15).	What matters is to evangelise man's culture and cultures (20). The task of evangelising all people constitutes the essential mission of the church ... her deepest identity. She exists in order to evangelise (14).	The gospel entrusted to us is also the word of truth. ... Every evangeliser is expected to have a reverence for ... revealed truth (78).	Evangelisation will ... always contain—as the foundation, centre, and ... summit of its dynamism—a clear proclamation that, in Jesus Christ, the Son of God made man, who died and rose from the dead, salvation is offered (27).	Salvation is offered to all men as a gift of God's grace and mercy (27). The church links human liberation and salvation in Jesus Christ, but she never identifies them (35). The church ... reaffirms the primacy of her spiritual vocation and refuses to replace the proclamation of the kingdom by the proclamation of forms of human liberation (34).
Nairobi 75: The distinctive lifestyle of Christians is this: While we are '' not of the world, even as he was not of the world, so we are also sent 'into' the world, just as he was sent into the world'' (I.4).	Christians are ... called to engage in both evangelism and social action. We are commissioned to proclaim the gospel of Christ to the ends of the earth. (I.3). The uncommunicated gospel is a patent contradiction (I.53).	There is great diversity in our confessions of Christ. Nevertheless ... we confess Christ as God and Saviour *according to the Scriptures* (I.24).	We are called to preach Christ crucified, the power of God, and the wisdom of God. Evangelism, therefore, is rooted in gratitude for God's self-sacrificing love, in obedience to the risen Lord (I.54, 55).	We boldly confess Christ alone as Saviour and Lord (I.1). We regret that some reduce liberation from sin and evil to social and political dimensions, just as we regret that others limit liberation to the private and eternal dimensions (I.19).

6	7	8	9	10
Conversion is demanded by the gospel	**True conversion invariably leads to costly discipleship**	**The whole church needs to be mobilised and trained for evangelism**	**The church can evangelise only when it is renewed**	**The power of the Holy Spirit is indispensable to evangelism**
The proclamation of Christ and the offer of salvation must lead to a summons to repent and believe, which is conversion.	*Although God's salvation is a free gift of his grace, it issues inevitably in a costly discipleship which must not be concealed by the evangelist.*	*Evangelism is a responsibility laid by Christ upon his whole church and every member of it. So the people of God must be both mobilised and trained.*	*The church can evangelise effectively only when it is renewed in its own life and unity, becomes an authentic embodiment of the gospel, and penetrates deeply into non-Christian society.*	*Evangelism is not just a human activity. Only the Holy Spirit can make the church's witness powerful and draw people to faith in Christ.*
Lausanne Covenant: To proclaim Jesus as "the Saviour of the world" ... is to proclaim God's love for a world of sinners and to invite all men to respond to him as Saviour and Lord in the wholehearted personal commitment of repentance and faith (3). Evangelism is the proclamation of ... Christ ... with a view of persuading people to come to him personally (4).	In issuing the gospel invitation we have no liberty to conceal the cost of discipleship. Jesus still calls all who would follow him to deny themselves, take up their cross, and identify themselves with his new community. (4). The salvation we claim should be transforming us in the totality of our personal and social responsibilities. Faith without works is dead (5).	The church is ... God's ... appointed means of spreading the gospel. ... World evangelisation requires the whole church to take the whole gospel to the whole world (6). In every nation and culture there should be an effective training programme for pastors and laymen (11).	Evangelism will become a realistic possibility only when the Spirit renews the church in truth and wisdom, faith, holiness, love, and power (14). A church which preaches the cross must itself be marked by the cross (6). Evangelism also summons us to unity because ... our disunity undermines our gospel of reconciliation (7). We need to break out of our ecclesiastical ghettos and permeate non-Christian society (6).	We believe in the power of the Holy Spirit. The Father sent his Spirit to bear witness to his Son: without his witness ours is futile ... we therefore call upon all Christians to pray for ... a visitation of the sovereign Spirit of God (14).
Evangelii Nuntiandi: The presentation of the gospel message ... is the	This kingdom and this salvation ... are available	The whole church is missionary, and the work of	For the church, the first means of evangelisation is	Evangelisation will never be possible without the ac-

duty incumbent on her (sc. the church) by the command of the Lord Jesus, so that people can believe and be saved (5). The respectful presentation of Christ and his kingdom is . . . the evangeliser's . . . duty with complete charity and with a total respect for the free options which it presents (80).	to every human being as grace and mercy, and yet at the same time each individual must gain them by force (cf. Matthew 11:12; Luke 16:16) . . . through toil and suffering . . . through abnegation and the cross . . . through a total interior renewal which the gospel calls *metanoia*; it is a radical conversion, a profound change of mind and heart (10).	evangelisation is a basic duty of the people of God (59). A serious preparation is needed for all workers of evangelisation (73).	the witness of an authentically Christian life, given over to God . . . and at the same time given to one's neighbour (41). Without this mark of holiness, our word will have difficulty in touching the heart of modern man (76). Unity among (Christ's) followers . . . is the test of the credibility of Christians and of Christ himself (77). The church . . . is the people of God immersed in the world (15).	tion of the Holy Spirit. . . . Techniques of evangelisation are good, but . . . could not replace the gentle action of the Spirit. . . . Without the Holy Spirit the most convincing dialectic has no power over the heart of man. . . . We exhort all evangelisers . . . to pray without ceasing to the Holy Spirit . . . and to let themselves prudently be guided by him (75).
Nairobi 75: The gospel always includes: the announcement of God's kingdom and love through Jesus Christ, the offer of grace and forgiveness of sins, the invitation to repentance and faith in him (1.57).	We deplore cheap conversions without consequences. We deplore a superficial gospel-preaching, an empty gospel without a call into personal and communal discipleship (1.14).	Evangelism . . . is entrusted to the "whole church," the body of Christ (1.61). Programmes of lay training ought to be encouraged (1.66).	Too often we as churches and congregations stand in the way of the gospel (1.63). The call to evangelism, therefore, implies a call to repentance, renewal, and commitment for visible unity (1.64). Authentic Christians live the death and resurrection of Christ by living the forgiven life in selfless service to others (47).	We believe with certainty in the presence and guidance of the Holy Spirit, who proceeds from the Father and bears witness to Christ. . . . Our witness to Christ is made strong in the Holy Spirit (1.11). We experience the power of the Holy Spirit to confess Christ in a life marked by both suffering and joy (1.5).

Reprinted by permission from *Third Way*, published by Thirty Press, Ltd. (in association with the Evangelical Alliance), 130 City Road, London EC1V 2NJ.

MESSAGE FROM MELBOURNE, 1980

Dear Sisters and Brothers in Christ:

We, more than five hundred Christians from many of the world's nations, have gathered in Melbourne, Australia, May 12-24, 1980, in the World Council of Churches' Conference on World Mission and Evangelism. In the name of Jesus Christ we have come. Our attention focused on the prayer Jesus taught us: "Your kingdom come." This prayer disturbs us and comforts us, yet by it we are united.

We meet under the clouds of nuclear threat and annihilation. Our world is deeply wounded by the oppressions inflicted by the powerful upon the powerless. These oppressions are found in our economic, political, racial, sexual, and religious life. Our world, so proud of human achievements, is full of people suffering from hunger, poverty, and injustice. People are wasted.

> Have they no knowledge, all the evildoers who eat up my people as they eat bread?
>
> (Psalm 14:4)

The poor and the hungry cry to God. Our prayer "Your kingdom come" must be prayed in solidarity with the cry of millions who are living in poverty and injustice. Peoples suffer the pain of silent torment; their faces reveal their suffering. The church cannot live distant from these faces because she sees the face of Jesus in them (Matthew 25).

In such a world the announcement of the kingdom of God comes to all. It comes to the poor and in them generates the power to affirm their human dignity, liberation, and hope. To the oppressor it comes as judgement, challenge and a call for repentance. To the insensitive it comes as a call to awareness of responsibility. The church itself has often failed its Lord by hindering the coming of his kingdom. We admit this sin and our need for repentance, forgiveness, and cleansing.

The triune God, revealed in the person and work of Jesus Christ, is the centre of all peoples and all things. Our Saviour Jesus Christ was laid in a manger "because there was no place for [him] . . . in the inn" (Luke 2:7). He is central to life yet moves towards those on the edge of life. He affirms his lordship by giving it up. He was crucified "outside the gate" (Hebrews 13:12). In this surrender of power he establishes his power to heal. The good news of the kingdom must be presented to the world by the church, the body of Christ, the sacrament of the kingdom in every place and time. It is through the power of the Holy Spirit that the kingdom is brought to its final consummation.

People who suffer injustice are on the periphery of national and community life. Multitudes are economically and politically oppressed. Often these are the people who have not heard of the gospel of Jesus Christ. But Jesus Christ comes to them. He exercises his healing authority on the periphery. We, participants in this Conference on World Mission and Evangelism, are challenged by the suffering of the poor. We pray that they may hear the gospel and that all of us may be worthy proclaimers of the gospel by word and life. We stand under the judgement and the hope of Jesus Christ. The prayer "Your kingdom come" brings us closer to Jesus Christ in today's world. We invite you to join us in commitment to the Lord for the coming of whose kingdom we pray.

Your kingdom come, O Lord!

Reprinted by permission from *International Review of Mission*, Geneva, Switzerland, Vol. LXIX, No. 275, July 1980.

THE THAILAND STATEMENT
From the Consultation on World Evangelization, August 1980 (A Follow-up to the Lausanne Congress of 1974)

Contents
Introduction: The Consultation on World Evangelization
The Mandate for World Evangelization
The Primacy of Evangelization
Some Vital Aspects of Evangelization
Cooperation in World Evangelization
Our Commitment to Christ

Introduction

We have gathered at Pattaya, Thailand, for the Consultation on World Evangelization, over 800 Christians from a wide diversity of backgrounds, nations, and cultures.

We have spent 10 days together in a fellowship of study, praise, and prayer. We have celebrated God's great love for us and for all humanity. We have considered before him and under his Word the command of our Lord Jesus Christ to proclaim the gospel to all people on earth. We have become freshly burdened by the vast numbers who have never heard the good news of Christ and are lost without him. We have been made ashamed of our failure to live out the gospel in its fulness, for these things have lessened our obedience and compromised our witness. We have noted that there are hard places where opposition is strong and evangelism is difficult. At the same time, we have rejoiced to hear how God is at work in his world, and how he is making many peoples receptive to his Word.

Our consultation has been held in the ancient Kingdom of Thailand, and we are grateful for the welcome which we have received from the hospitable Thai people. In particular we have enjoyed fellowship with Thai church leaders, and have sought to share the concern of their hearts that, after more than 150 years of Protestant missions, considerably less than one percent of their country's 46 million people confess Jesus Christ as Saviour and Lord.

Close by, on the country's eastern border, are hundreds of thousands of refugees from neighboring countries. They symbolize both the political ferment of the world and the tragic suffering of millions of human beings. We denounce the injustice of which they are victims, and have struggled to understand and feel their plight. We thank God for those Christians who have been among the first to go to their aid. We thank him also that growing numbers of them, uprooted from their ancestral homes and cultural inheritance, are finding in Jesus Christ a new security and a new life.

We have made a solemn resolution to involve ourselves more actively in the relief and rehabilitation of refugees throughout the world.

The Mandate for World Evangelization

We believe that there is only one living and true God, the Creator of the universe and the Father of our Lord Jesus Christ; that he has made all men, women, and children in his own likeness; that he loves all those whom he has made, although they have rebelled against him and are under his judgment; and that he longs for their salvation. He sent his Son Jesus Christ to die for sinners and, having raised him from the dead, has given him universal authority, that every knee should bow to him and every tongue confess him Lord. This exalted Jesus now sends us, on whom he has had mercy, into the world as his witnesses and servants.

As his witnesses he has commanded us to proclaim his good news in the power of the Holy Spirit to every person of every culture and nation, and to summon them to repent, to believe, and to follow him. This mandate is urgent, for there is no other Saviour but Jesus Christ. It is also binding on all Christian people. As the Lausanne Covenant declares, the evangelistic task "requires the whole church to take the whole gospel to the whole world" (para. 6).

We are also the servants of Jesus Christ who is himself both "the servant" and "the Lord." He calls us, therefore, not only to obey him as Lord in every area of our lives, but also to serve as he served. We confess that we have not sufficiently followed his example of love in identifying with the poor and hungry, the deprived, and the oppressed. Yet all God's people "should share his concern for justice and reconciliation throughout human society and for the liberation of men from every kind of oppression" (Lausanne Covenant, para. 5).

Although evangelism and social action are not identical, we gladly reaffirm our commitment to both, and we endorse the Lausanne Covenant in its entirety. It remains the basis of our common activity, and nothing it contains is beyond our concern, so long as it is clearly related to world evangelization.

The Primacy of Evangelization

The Lausanne Covenant declares that "in the church's mission of sacrificial service evangelism is primary" (para. 6). This is not to deny that evangelism and social action are integrally related, but rather to acknowledge that of all the tragic needs of human beings none is greater than their alienation from their Creator and the terrible reality of eternal death for those who refuse to repent and believe. If therefore we do not commit ourselves with urgency to the task of evangelization, we are guilty of an inexcusable lack of human compassion.

Some two thirds of the world's four and a half billion people have had no proper opportunity to receive Christ. We have considered the value of thinking of them not only as individuals but also as "people groups" who perceive themselves as having an affinity with one another. Many are within easy reach of Christians. Large numbers of these are already Christian in name, yet still need to be evangelized because they have not understood the gospel or not responded to it. The great majority of people in the world, however, have no Christian neighbors to share Christ with them. They can therefore be reached only by cross-cultural messengers of the gospel. We confidently expect that these will increasingly come from all countries, as the Christian mission becomes universalized, and we will work to keep this challenge before the churches.

Some Vital Aspects of Evangelization

At Lausanne our theme was "Let the earth hear his voice"; in Thailand it has been "How shall they hear?" So we have searched the Scriptures daily in order to learn more about the God who speaks, the message he has spoken, and the people to whom and through whom he speaks.

We have reaffirmed our confidence in the truth and power of God's Word, and our desire to let his voice penetrate our cultural defences. We have recognized the local church as the principal agency for evangelism, whose total membership must therefore be mobilized and trained. We have heard the call to be sensitive to other people's cultural patterns and not to try to impose on them our own. We have also acknowledged the indispensable necessity of the work of the Holy Spirit, and of prayer to the sovereign Lord for boldness to speak for him.

For five of our ten days together we have divided into 17 mini-consultations, all of which have concentrated on how to reach particular peoples for Christ. These mini-consultations have built upon a lengthy study program in which hundreds of groups throughout the world have been involved. Our purpose has been to consider important issues of theology and methodology, in relation to our approach to different peoples, in order to develop realistic strategies for evangelism.

Many of the reports have called for a change in our personal attitudes. The following four have been particularly emphasized:

The first is *love*. Group after group has asserted that "we cannot evangelize if we do not love." We have had to repent of prejudice, disrespect, and even hostility towards the very people we want to reach for Christ. We have also resolved to love others as God in Christ has loved us, and to identify with them in their situation as he identified himself with us in ours.

Second, *humility*. Our study has led us to confess that other people's resistance to the gospel has sometimes been our fault. Imperialism, slavery, religious persecution in the name of Christ, racial pride, and prejudice (whether anti-black or anti-white, anti-Jewish or anti-Arab, or any other kind), sexual oppression, cultural insensitivity, and indifference to the plight of the needy and the powerless—these are some of the evils which have marred the church's testimony and put stumbling blocks in other people's road to faith. We resolve in future to spread the gospel with greater humility.

Third, *integrity*. Several groups have written about the character and conduct of the message-bearer. Our witness loses credibility when we contradict it by our life or lifestyle. Our light will shine only when others can see our good works (Mt. 5:16). In a word, if we are to speak of Jesus with integrity, we have to resemble him.

The fourth emphasis has to do with *power*. We know that we are engaged in a spiritual battle with demonic forces. Evangelism often involves a power encounter, and in conversion Jesus Christ demonstrates that he is stronger than the strongest principalities and powers of evil by liberating their victims. Strategy and organization are not enough; we need to pray earnestly for the power of the Holy Spirit. God has not given us a spirit of fear, but of boldness.

Cooperation in World Evangelization

We have been deeply concerned during our consultation to strengthen evangelical cooperation in global evangelization, for no single agency could accomplish this enormous task alone.

We joyfully affirm the unity of the body of Christ and acknowledge that we are bound together with one another and with all true believers. While a true unity in Christ is not necessarily incompatible with organizational diversity, we must nevertheless strive for a visible expression of our oneness. This witnesses to Christ's reconciling power and demonstrates our common commitment to serve him. In contrast, competitive programmes and needless duplication of effort both waste resources and call into question our profession to be one in Christ. So we pledge ourselves again, in the words of the Lausanne Covenant, "to seek a deeper unity in truth, worship, holiness, and mission" (para. 7).

It is imperative that we work together to fulfill the task of world evangelization. Cooperation must never be sought at the expense of basic biblical teahing, whether doctrinal or ethical. At the same time, disagreement on nonessentials among those equally concerned to submit to Scripture should not prevent cooperation in evangelism. Again, cooperation must never inhibit the exercise of the diverse gifts and ministries which the Holy Spirit gives to the people of God. Nor should the diversity of gifts and ministries be made an excuse for noncooperation.

Yet obstacles to cooperation remain, which involve genuine problems and complex issues. Some of these reflect either the social, political, geographical, and cultural circumstances or the ecclesiastical traditions from which we come. Others reflect tensions between different forms of ministry (e.g., between traditional church structures and those which are not directly accountable to churches) or between different evangelistic strategies and methodologies. These and other tensions are real and must be frankly faced. They do not release us, however, from our responsibility to explore with creativity different levels of cooperation in evangelism. We are determined to work more closely together. The Scripture urges us to "stand firm in one spirit, with one mind, striving side by side for the faith of the gospel" (Phil. 1:27).

We believe that God has given a special role to the Lausanne Committee for World Evangelization to act as a catalyst for world evangelization. We desire therefore to give it a further mandate to stimulate evangelism throughout the world, on the basis of the Lausanne Covenant, and in growing cooperation with others of like mind.

Our Commitment to Christ

In the light of his clear command to go and make disciples of all nations, his universal authority, and his love for all humanity, we solemnly make the following commitment to Christ, which we shall seek his grace to fulfill:

1. We pledge ourselves to *live* under the lordship of Christ, and to be concerned for his will and his glory, not our own.
2. We pledge ourselves to *work* for the evangelization of the world, and to bear witness by word and deed to Christ and his salvation.
3. We pledge ourselves to *serve* the needy and the oppressed, and in the name of Christ to seek for them relief and justice.
4. We pledge ourselves to *love* all those we are called to serve, even as Christ loved us, and to identify with them.
5. We pledge ourselves to *pray* for the church and for the world, that Christ will renew his church in order to reach his world.

6. We pledge ourselves to *study* God's Word, to seek Christ in it, and to relate it to ourselves and our contemporaries.

7. We pledge ourselves to *give* with the generosity of Christ, that we may share with others what he has given to us.

8. We pledge ourselves to *go* wherever Christ may send us, and never to settle down so comfortably that we cannot contemplate a move.

9. We pledge ourselves to *labour* to mobilize Christ's people, so that the whole church may take the whole gospel to the whole world.

10. We pledge ourselves to *cooperate* with all who share with us the true gospel of Christ, in order to reach the unreached peoples of the world.

11. We pledge ourselves to *seek* the power of the Spirit of Christ, that he may fill us and flow through us.

12. We pledge ourselves to *wait* with eagerness for Christ's return, and to be busy in his service until he comes.

We believe that God, who has uniquely exalted his Son Jesus Christ, has led us to make these pledges to him. With hope and prayer we invite all Christ's followers to join us in our commitment, so that we may work together for the evangelization of the world.

Issued at the Consultation on World Evangelization, Pattaya, Thailand, June 1980. Used with permission of the Lausanne Committee for World Evangelization.

Missionary Study Series

Published by Herald Press, Scottdale, Pennsylvania, in association with the Institute of Mennonite Studies, Elkhart, Indiana.

1. *The Challenge of Church Growth.* A symposium edited by Wilbert R. Shenk with contributions also from John H. Yoder, Allan H. Howe, Robert L. Ramseyer, and J. Stanley Friesen (1973).

2. *Modern Messianic Movements, As a Theological and Missionary Challenge* by Gottfried Oosterwal (1973).

3. *From Kuku Hill: Among Indigenous Churches in West Africa* by Edwin and Irene Weaver (1975).

4. *Bibliography of Henry Venn's Printed Writings with Index* by Wilbert R. Shenk (1975).

5. *Christian Mission and Social Justice* by Samuel Escobar and John Driver (1978).

6. *A Spirituality of the Road* by David J. Bosch (1979).

7. *Mission and the Peace Witness: The Gospel and Christian Discipleship.* A symposium edited by Robert L. Ramseyer with contributions also from James E. Metzler, Marlin E. Miller, Richard Showalter, Ronald J. Sider, Sjouke Voolstra, and John H. Yoder (1979).

8. *Letters Concerning the Spread of the Gospel in the Heathen World* by Samuel S. Haury (1981).

9. *Evangelizing Neopagan North America* by Alfred C. Krass (1982).

The Missionary Study Series grows out of the Mennonite Missionary Study Fellowship (MMSF) program. The MMSF is an informal fellowship of persons interested in Christian mission, meeting annually for a three-day conference on issues central to their task. It includes missionaries, mission board administrators, theologians, sociologists, and others. It is sponsored by the Institute of Mennonite Studies (IMS), 3003 Benham Avenue, Elkhart, Ind. 46517. Books in the series may be ordered from Provident Bookstores, 616 Walnut Avenue, Scottdale, Pa. 15683.

Alfred C. Krass is a minister of the United Church of Christ. Ever since he first went to Ghana as a missionary in 1961, he has had an ardent desire to understand other peoples and their culture and to seek to find creative ways to communicate the gospel to them.

At present he lives with his family in the Germantown section of Philadelphia, a multiracial neighborhood that he describes as "a beehive of activity." As vice-president for Economic and Community Development of his neighborhood association, and as a member of the Economic Development Committee of the Philadelphia Council of Neighborhood Organizations, he seeks to work with others to create new jobs and industries.

Krass is supported in his ministry by his house church, Jubilee Fellowship, which sees his work as part of their holistic outreach to the city. Krass has authored several tracts and uses these and other means to communicate the gospel as he works on behalf of human justice.

Long involved in international concerns, Krass pursues these interests as an active board member of Jubilee Fund and American Christians for the Abolition of Torture.

Krass's present activities are quite a switch from his earlier involvements in academic life, writing and speaking, and the church bureaucracy. He says he has no regrets about the time he spent in those pursuits, but "I needed to get back to the testing ground, to the place of encounter between faith and lack of faith."

Born in Brooklyn, N.Y., and educated at Amherst College, Yale Divinity School, the universities of Edinburgh and Basel, and the New School for Social Research, Krass describes himself as "a lifelong reader of the Bible." In this book he tells where his reading of the Scriptures "in context" has led him.

Krass is editor-at-large of *The Other Side* magazine. His wife, Susan, is managing editor of the Lutheran mission publication, *World Encounter.*